MIND IC

Notes on Intellectual Capital Management

Robin,

Thanks very much for all your hard work in our intellectual capital management group and for your heroic support of LES Standards.

Bill Elkington

Bill Elkington

MIND IC
Notes on Intellectual Capital Management

Outskirts Press, Inc.
http://www.outskirtspress.com

ISBN: 978-1-9772-3838-2

The image on the front cover is taken from one of Diego Rivera's series of frescos—entitled Detroit Industry, created in 1932 and 1933—in the courtyard of the Detroit Institute of Arts and is provided with permission of the Institute. This panel is from the North Wall and depicts the Ford signature innovation—the use of the overhead trolley—a moving assembly line system first employed at Ford Motor Company's Highland Park plant, in the manufacture of the Model T.

Credit: Diego M. Rivera, Detroit Industry, North Wall, 1932-1933, fresco. Detroit Institute of Arts, Gift of Edsel B. Ford, 33.10.N.

In research, as in the whole civilizing process,
why does it take so long to learn so little?

—Edwin H. Land

Quoted by Ronald K. Fierstein in
A Triumph of Genius: Edwin Land,
Polaroid, and the Kodak Patent War
(Ankerwycke 2015)

Praise for
MIND IC: Notes on Intellectual Capital

A pioneer in intellectual capital management and strategy, Bill Elkington provides an indispensable framework for any business manager to protect—and enhance—enterprise value through the proactive management of intangible business assets.

—**Kevin Arst:** Senior Managing Partner, Ankura Consulting Group

A visionary book making a compelling case that we all need to be more mindful of intellectual capital (IC). IC is everywhere—the better an entity understands it, the more value it can extract for its shareholders and reduce risk. This is a concise and practical handbook on IC that can catalyze the implementation of these ideas at enterprise level.

—**Mihaela D. Bojin:** Associate Director, University of Iowa
Research Foundation

This book is for every intellectual property professional who has been frustrated by the challenges of communicating the importance of IP to C-suite level executives. Bill Elkington will get you out of your comfort zone and lead you on a journey to mastery of the true value of your company's intellectual capital—a new paradigm for broadly framing and defining traditional and emerging forms of IP that will cover the waterfront of your company's value proposition to customers, partners, and investors. The text is interlaced with Bill's trademark wit and storytelling wisdom, producing a thoroughly enjoyable read.

—**Gillian Fenton:** Senior Counsel, Vaccines Legal Operations, GSK

Bill Elkington brings to light the silent challenge facing many companies today—managing one of the most valuable corporate assets, intellectual capital. A significant driver of enterprise value, it is not measured by traditional accounting practices and is not understood by many in leadership positions. Mind IC provides a new perspective on information-age business and a playbook for managing a company's most relevant assets.

—**Scott Williams:** Vice President, GE Licensing, General Electric

Contents

Foreword

I was astounded, while reading this book, by how much it reflected my own professional journey. I am a patent attorney (and at times a business founder) who over 25 years has shifted from making intellectual *property* (IP) increasingly relevant to the businesses I advise or build, to appreciating the essential role of intellectual *capital* (and not just IP) to those businesses. This book identifies the common flaws of those who have at times overlooked adequate management of intellectual capital (which goes far beyond legal protections such as IP rights). And most importantly, this book identifies existing intellectual capital solutions that many of us have seen leaders successfully develop and which others can now implement quickly.

In reaction to IP-centric views, business executives would say "the business drives the business." What they meant was that front-office business *needs* (for, say, future cash flows) are dependent on business *decisions*, and should therefore be more influential than some back-office accounting or legal preferences. So those business decisions should be driven primarily by the crucial business needs rather than secondary guidelines or aspirations. They also would say "there is no revenue without some amount of risk." The key is to find the right balance, and the commerce-oriented executives should be the decision-makers, rather than the lawyers or accountants.

While the primacy of commercial needs remains chiefly the same today, the world's economies and businesses have been changing at the fastest rate in human history. And yet our commercial practices, processes, standards, and measurements of business value have not kept pace with those changes. This is particularly true as businesses shift from reliance on tangible assets to intangible assets and the intellectual capital that catalyzes that value.

Today, new multi-billion-dollar businesses are being created that intentionally have very few physical assets, and so intellectual capital and intangible assets are therefore an increasingly important component of commercial value and risk. And while not all companies have adapted, some demonstrate strong intellectual capital and intangible asset management that are embodied in their strategies, which provide excellent lessons.

For example, many legacy businesses may now be increasingly reliant on "material" changes to their business models such as moving from a costly distribution of goods via retail stores to an online platform that provides just-in-time inventory. These types of changes yield different measures of success-factors in the present economy. The intellectual capital, which resides and sometimes hides in our relationships, innovations, and competitive differentiation, is now an ever-increasingly important aspect of value and risk for companies.

However, unlike in prior times where enterprises have adapted and adopted contributions of other professional advisors, it is now past due for specialists in the intellectual capital profession to unlock the raw potential within the intellectual capital value-chain. This is especially true in our age of the knowledge-economy, which introduces unique ways to deliver value in our mobility-connected, internet-based and data-driven world. This has led to a disjointed (or lack of) discussion between business executives, accountants, and attorneys, whereby each addresses only part of a larger and more robust whole…that is, until the publication of this ground-breaking book.

This book's unique approach begins to solve the communication break-downs by unifying stakeholders under a comprehensive intellectual capital discussion framework. The approach taken uses common business language rather than legalese or accountant-speak, along with meaningful analogies embodied in famous quotes and anecdotes. The result is refreshingly full of life, instead of what might otherwise be difficult to understand and master.

Present-day issues surrounding intellectual capital are rooted in simpler times when managing an enterprise meant dealing mainly with tangible assets. This book recognizes that a newly honed awareness is needed for healthier intellectual capital management, which it delivers. This book also offers both paradigm shifts and gentle nudges to remedy prior deficiencies, by respectfully encouraging (rather than criticizing) all involved in their pursuit of doing their best for their companies and professions.

What is perhaps among the most valuable aspects of this book is the practical guidance it provides. It shines a brilliant light on intellectual capital and highlights the benefits of and ways to create a unifying culture around identifying, valuing, and commercializing that intellectual capital. Further advances are suggested by using change management to propagate the adjustments, and utilizing metrics to identify and report on the progress being made.

This book provides quite literally a pivotal approach that now gives us clearer insight into what has been unendurable in prior approaches around respecting and appropriately commercializing intellectual capital. Its guidance therefore simultaneously points us in a more prosperous direction to the benefit of our companies, our customers, our partners, our professions, and global society at large. This book is a game-changer by being "the" conversation-starter and script for tackling today's intellectual capital-centric economy!

Paul Roberts,
2021 Chair, Intellectual Assets in the Boardroom
Committee of LES Standards

Preface

These notes are few—to respect the reader's time. I try to make my point and move on quickly. But this little book is also ambitious; it means to say some consequential things about what one can do to manage companies' most valuable asset class significantly better.

It's more practical than theoretical. And by the way, expect no scholarship here. I'm no scholar.

The intent is to introduce a variety of people from a great diversity of academic and experiential backgrounds—people who may now regard themselves first and foremost as business-people—to a different way of thinking about what most of us business-people do most of the time in companies—at least in most companies, in most industries.

My career has been in aerospace and defense; as a result, some of the illustrative examples and references are chosen from that industry. But this essay should be relevant to any enterprise that is collaborative and must—of necessity—share (either under a non-disclosure agreement, full-blown license, or assignment or joint ownership agreement) a significant amount of intellectual capital across enterprise boundaries with government agencies, customers, suppliers, consortium partners, joint ventures, joint venture partners, standards setting work groups, and co-development partners, for example.

And let me be clear, my view is that a substantial portion of the economy is characterized by tightly-coupled business-to-business supply chains and collaborative networks in which the attempted coercion and theft and misuse of intellectual capital rights occurs routinely, to the detriment of both innovation and the flowering of the economy. Businesses and other entities (such as government agencies) with asymmetrical market power (whether manifested through financial power or intellectual capital power asymmetries, or both) routinely attempt (often with remarkable success) to coerce unusual intellectual capital rights from their business partners for something considerably less than the value of those rights, capturing a remarkable percentage of the value of the investments and innovations of others for themselves.

(A confirming piece of information for this claim—outside of my own personal experience and the reported personal experience of other colleagues—is the following. I participated in a benchmarking study conducted by a major accounting and consulting firm a number of years ago. The participants represented a wide variety of industries. Perhaps as many as a dozen companies and industries participated. The industry sectors that I remember were the following: oil and gas, chemicals, electronics, telecommunications, automotive, software, and aerospace & defense.

There were a few others, I believe, but I don't recall what they were.)

(The benchmarking was on the subject of intellectual capital management or what the benchmarking firm called intellectual property management. One of the areas probed was the level of perceived risk to a company's intellectual capital, through coercion of rights or the theft of rights. The number one source of intellectual capital rights risk across these different industries was perceived to be a company's business partners. Remarkably, the companies represented in the study were themselves quite large, as I recall, ranging from $5B to $25B or more per year in sales.)

My view is also that a significant threat that many companies face is from competitor business model innovation and the rapid reconfiguration of enterprises from being hardware-and-engineering-services-centric to being software-and-information/data-services-centric. Many medium and large enterprises today have billions of dollars of investment in business processes—whether instantiated in software or not—that enable them to compete effectively. Many such enterprises find themselves going to market increasingly with software-and-information/data-based products and services. But they often do not have a systematic way of understanding how to manage the value of these business processes and intangible products and services. Their key metrics are often geared to a hardware-and-engineering-services business model, and this means that when transactions of various kinds come along in the intangibles realm—whether for business processes (e.g. joint ventures) or technology or intangible products and services, whether software, data/information, or access-based—they may potentially be caught flat-footed.

Companies outside of these two groups may also benefit from what I am about to say—companies with related or unrelated vulnerabilities, such as: (1) supply chain or supply network exposure to theft and misuse of proprietary information, (2) a lack of clarity around the relative value of different intellectual capital rights bundles, (3) a lack of standards knowledge and best practices understanding in establishing and managing relationships based on intellectual capital rights exchanges, (4) lack of intangibles valuation expertise, (5) a lack of a quantitative understanding of intellectual capital investment productivity, (6) unclear responsibilities and authorities around pricing of intellectual capital rights, (7) lack of systematic management approaches to intellectual capital, (8) absence of integrated thinking and planning relating to business strategy and intellectual capital strategy, (9) little education and awareness across the enterprise of the roles, responsibilities, tools, metrics, and training pertaining to the management of the enterprise's intellectual capital engines and stores.

This book is meant to help companies that find themselves in these circumstances and to offer some thoughts about how to structure company thinking, organization, skill, and focus to address these vulnerabilities.

In addition, companies that buy and/or sell product lines, need expert help with transfer pricing, or want to set up strategic partner channels or joint ventures globally to address out-of-reach markets may find these ideas useful, along with others.

The value of companies today is mostly in their intellectual capital store and the creative engines that build and replenish that store. Many of the sorts of companies described above should, therefore, find some of the suggestions here helpful.

This book is definitely not about legal matters, but lawyers may find it interesting.

I mean these notes to get at some of the more urgent issues that I have seen in intellectual capital management in the companies with which I'm familiar. It's not intended to be comprehensive. It's not oceanic in scope. It is not meant to cover all of the key areas of intellectual capital management that a company might want to attend to—just the several that have jumped out at me as I've made my way through my career. It is not meant to be theoretical. And it is not meant to explore public policy issues. It may be a bit eccentric in its style and approach. (I may come across, for example, as a bit of a Woody Woodpecker rattling around in a Mickey Mouse cartoon.) It may be a bit silly from time to time.

This essay is focused on what business-people who have some understanding of intellectual capital and its management can do—what they might consider doing if they want to make a valuable difference in their companies. I look only for the low hanging fruit and pick that; a more wide-ranging and thorough treatment of the subject would likely provide more action items for intellectual capital managers to pursue. But in the early stages of changing the way an enterprise approaches managing its intellectual capital, the suggested areas of focus will tend to elicit less resistance and therefore be more successful.

I suggest that there should be an organization populated by intellectual capital management experts leading the work in this field for companies. In small companies, such an organization should be small. In large companies, such an organization should be larger. Without any business group leading the business and financial management of this important area, what we have is *ad hoc* management of companies' intellectual capital. This is suboptimal.

The endeavor here is to provide a somewhat different perspective on intellectual capital management and to provide some suggestions as to how business leaders may make their intellectual capital investments more productive, in the normal course of business.

The observations in this book should be relevant to both large and small businesses, since intellectual capital matters a great deal to most enterprises today, regardless of their size.

I argue for a quantitative more than a qualitative orientation. But I don't ignore qualitative approaches. Cross-enterprise business policy and process design and maintenance is just as much a part of intellectual capital management as is quantitative analysis and decision-making based on quantitative analysis.

I assume that we are tending to our knitting, attending mainly to the business of offering products and services. It is in this context that we will do our work here. There is nothing odd or exotic: just tips on what we can do in the normal course of our business to add value through managing intellectual capital better.

This book is not about patent licensing. Patent licensing is mentioned, but only in passing. And it is not specifically about licensing of other kinds of intellectual capital, although licensing of intellectual capital rights is one of the important areas of intellectual capital management that is considered.

In other words, it is not focused on licensing technology or patents or trademarks as a business. It is focused on companies pursuing conventional business models: selling products and services, whether tangible, intangible, or some hybrid of the two. Again, its concern is with conventional operating companies and the strategic intellectual capital risks and opportunities they have.

This book is also not about early stage technology licensing, although early stage technology licensing is not excluded.

This essay is directed at business-people in operating companies, principally, but my colleagues in university technology transfer offices may find it interesting as well, along with procurement and regulatory people in US agencies. It is really directed at the sort of cross-disciplinary heroes that I have run into often in my volunteer work with the Licensing Executives Society, USA and Canada (LES). These are people who might have a PhD in chemical engineering or anthropology or philosophy or electrical engineering. People who might be medical doctors or MBAs or accounting and finance professors. Professional investors and serial entrepreneurs. PhD economists and computer scientists and manufacturing engineers and historians and linguists. Inventors of all stripes. And more.

The concept of intellectual capital management advanced here is transaction-centric, because that is where I've found the easiest and quickest payoff for someone knowledgeable about intellectual capital and its quantitative value. Are there other important areas to explore? Sure. One could focus on stimulating creation of new intellectual capital platforms for growth or on re-deploying core competency intellectual capital from one market to another. One could focus on business processes designed to optimize one's performance in these areas. There are of course other areas of importance.

So this essay is focused, primarily, on an area of intellectual capital management that one might call a "blue ocean," in many companies. An area in which business and financial expertise in intellectual capital management can be applied with readily understandable benefits.

These notes are written for people who are stimulated by learning new things and who are interested in reaching across the boundaries of the various academic disciplines toward an understanding of intellectual capital and its management. I'm imagining an audience of polymaths, of people who want to understand how to manage operating companies better.

A note on tone: A friend, upon reading a version of this text, remarked that I seemed to be naïve. That I seemed not to understand that people at work are driven by power, politics, and a desire to control their own scope of work and the scope of work of others. And that I seemed to believe (naively) that by appealing to the better natures of my business colleagues, I could move the needle.

Look, I've been at the work of intellectual capital management for decades at several different Fortune 500 companies—work that has entailed changing the hearts and minds and thinking and rewards and behavior of people involved in intellectual capital management. I know that power, politics, and control are prevalent motives. I know that some people really don't care all that much about the long-term health of their companies, and I know that some people want to do their work without thinking much about it, collect their paychecks, and go home.

But I also do know that most people create purpose through their work, create meaning through their work. Some people, in addition to collecting a paycheck, feel good about themselves through accomplishing something they regard as beneficial in their work. Many of my work colleagues over the years have seemed to regard work as one important means by which they contribute to the human enterprise.

But please don't get any funny ideas about my having delusions about organizational behavior. I could write an encyclopedia on what doesn't work in intellectual capital management because of my colleagues' mixed motives and self-centeredness and resistance to change of any kind over the decades. I could teach a full set of graduate courses on what does not work in change management in operating companies pertaining to intellectual capital management.

But I won't. Instead, I'll distill what I've learned from decades of mistakes into a few things you can do to pull off a coup in how your company manages its intellectual capital.

A comment on style and structure: this little book is notational and perhaps elliptical. It is a set of thoughts on the subject of intellectual capital management, rather than being a big deal argument or a grand plan or a neat scheme or template by which to manage intellectual capital. It does not progress from A to B to C and to D. Rather, it may very well start with C and then move on to Q, only to return to K and then skip to the big W.

Random, you might say. Or maybe pseudo-random.

A note on lingo. I use the term "intellectual capital" intentionally, and I differentiate it from "intellectual property." I go into the differences in Chapter Two and into why I make the distinctions I make. (It is to achieve more clarity and less fog as we try to sort through this murky subject matter.) But I don't want this to be a book on the taxonomy of corporate non-tangibles. I don't want it to be adamantine in any way. It's purpose, once again, is to be suggestive of things that a business and financial person might do to improve the financial performance and value of his company. The focus is on the transactions and business relationships a company must execute and maintain, in the normal activities of developing and selling and supporting products and services, whether they be tangible, intangible, or a combination of the two.

Another note on lingo. I use the term "intellectual capital rights," and I differentiate them from "intellectual property rights." What can I possibly mean? By "intellectual property rights," I mean the legal rights a company may have by virtue of the application of intellectual property law (e.g. patent, copyright, trademark, and trade secret law) to a subset of one's intellectual capital. By "intellectual capital rights," I mean these legal rights and such things, for example, as the professional skill and know-how of a company's people, its brand, its culture and its related undocumented business processes, the nature and quality of its business relationships, contractual rights of various kinds, and causes of action. Does this category include legal rights? Yes. It also includes rights a company has by virtue of its control or influence over various sorts of intellectual capital within its orbit.

So by the term "rights," I don't mean necessarily to imply "effective" legal rights, because in my view, one may often have legal rights without their having any "effective" financial meaning. Whereas, when I talk about intellectual capital rights, I often think and talk about such rights as bundles of rights—bundles that may include intellectual property rights, other sorts of legal rights, and other sorts of rights—rights of control and influence. These latter rights may be possessed by a company as the result of its investment choices, relationship capital choices, structural capital choices, and human capital choices. These non-legal rights may be more "effective" financially than a company's legal rights, taken by themselves. Taken together these non-legal rights (rights of control and influence) may give a company a time advantage or other significant advantages in the marketplace. I discuss this further in Chapter Two.

And one more thing: I do respect everyone. Some of the people I consider here have had some difficulty with change and with expanding their knowledge and understanding of intellectual capital management. This is how all of us operate. We all have difficulty learning new things and with agreeing to change the nature of our work. This is a description of me as much as it is a description of some others I have worked with.

(We wouldn't have the fields of organizational behavior and change management, if most people operated with a significantly different behavioral bias.)

I give examples of this resistance here to make sure you understand the nature of the task, in many companies. There is some conflict and resistance to be expected when attempting to implement what I'm advocating. I want you to understand it and to be prepared for it and to have some approaches worked out to deal with it. And I do try to find the humor in all of this as well. After all, sapiens is a mighty odd and conflicted and objectively funny species!

In any event, I believe there are ideas in here that you can put to use to make your company significantly better and more valuable.

Chapter One:
Why You Should Read These Notes

Most organizations exploit only a fraction of the knowledge, experience, and intellectual capital that is available to them.
—**Patrick Lencioni:** The Advantage

A Very Short Story: A man walks through the door with a gun. In this case, the gun is metaphorical. It is a literary device. The man is a business-man and has been for 25 years. This is a real story. It really happened, in a metaphorical sense. The man is a good man, a conscientious man. A man, mind you, who is smart. He has an engineering degree and an MBA from a prestigious university. He knows product development, product management, and business processes around offering complex, custom-engineered products to customers and managing those products through their life-cycle. He is an expert in these business processes. He teaches others about these business processes. And yet, he walks through a door with a gun. He tells about a dozen others assembled around a conference table somewhere in the United States that licensing intellectual capital is a rare event in their company. It isn't part of their company's normal business processes. In saying this, he has fired his gun. It happens to be an omni-directional shotgun—a cartoon shotgun. He lets loose at everyone around the table with it. Then someone—someone who specializes in intellectual capital management—exercises her superpowers, stops the pellets mid-air and disarms him by saying, "Well Clive, we actually do license a great deal of intellectual capital when we sell our products. For example, throughout the requirements development and specification development processes with our customers, suppliers, and co-development partners, we license the know-how of our technologists, who help our business partners successfully develop their product designs, so that our products will be successful when integrated with theirs. We license the software embedded in our products and the documentation—our proprietary information—needed by customers to integrate our products into higher level assemblies. During product development, we often license software models of our products to our customers so that they can do model-based development of their higher-level systems. And during the development process, we will usually license interface information so that co-development partners can do their developments in parallel. And at any given point in time, we are participating in the development of about 75 technical standards and about half a dozen to a dozen business process standards, and in all of this standards work, we license our intellectual capital or promise to do so." Clive feels like he has been transported into the fictional world of *The Hitchhiker's Guide to the Galaxy*. There, he imagines himself to be Arthur Dent, one of two last surviving humans following the destruction of the earth by the Vogons, who have made way for a hyperspace bypass. Clive is speechless. Clive's lower jaw seems to dangle down around his penny loafers. He drifts aimlessly across the universe, wondering what he will do now that the world that he knew has been obliterated. Silence has descended on the conference room like an invasion of dark matter.

The moral of this story? Perhaps it is this: very knowledgeable, diligent, conscientious, and intelligent business-people do not understand fundamental matters concerning the management of the corporation's most valuable asset class: intellectual capital. This is inexcusable. We must find a way to address this issue effectively.

There are several reasons that reading this book will be worthwhile for business-people.

First, some (perhaps many) business-people are not used to thinking about the intellectual capital assets of their enterprise as, in fact, business assets. This essay will help people to do so. And since intellectual capital assets represent 60-90 percent of enterprise equity value, recognizing and managing these assets better has the promise of enhancing the enterprise's value significantly. (My claim that intellectual capital represents 60-90 percent of most companies' equity value is verified by many sources, one of which I reference later in the book.)

For example, let's say that you can improve your company's return on its intellectual capital assets by 20 percent over a period of several years. If your company's equity value starts at $10 billion, and its intellectual capital assets are worth $8 billion, then you should easily be able to increase your company's equity value by $1.6 billion. This means that your intellectual capital management work and innovation can result in an increase in your company's equity value by 16 percent.

That's pretty good for a few years' work!

How would you go about doing that, you might ask. There are many levers here. Read on to learn more about them.

Second, companies find themselves in the midst of transactions constantly—with customers, suppliers, government agencies, joint venture partners, universities, and co-development partners, for example—transactions in which intellectual capital is at the heart of things. And in many industries, the asymmetric market power of some players (e.g. customers, suppliers (surprisingly often), co-development partners, and government agencies) emboldens them to attempt to coerce (through the use of their "leverage" or perceived superior market power) commercially unusual rights to business partner intellectual capital, whether structural capital only or a combination of human capital, relationship capital, and structural capital. This is because most companies don't have the in-house capability to value the various equities of the intellectual capital bundles in question.

They don't have the learning and experience in quantitative analysis of intellectual capital rights, and they are therefore at a disadvantage when it comes to negotiating the business and financial terms of those relationships and agreements. They don't keep track of the developing and developed intellectual capital throughout the resulting collaborative relationships, and the result is that many intellectual capital bundles are not documented and conveyed according to the originating agreement.

Many companies undervalue their intellectual capital contributions to such relationships, thus sub-optimizing their returns on their intellectual capital investments. Understanding this and understanding how to do this valuation work in an objective manner turns out, therefore, to be a critical enterprise competency. This essay will help you understand this better and will point you to resources you can access to improve your knowledge and capability in this area.

Third, most companies lose a great deal of value in their intellectual capital (proprietary information, specifically) through attacks by competitors on their supply chain partners or other business partners. In other words, competitors steal intellectual capital that companies have placed in the hands of their suppliers and other business partners. These notes will point you to where to find best practices in this important area to reduce the risk of this happening.

Fourth, many companies make a serious category mistake, when it comes to the topic of intellectual capital management. Most companies think the lawyers have this area handled. They don't. Yes, the lawyers do own the business processes by which legal protections are applied to the company's intellectual capital, but they usually have less to do with all the non-legal business and financial processes that the company uses or can use to manage both the risk and value concerning the company's intangibles. These notes will help you understand how this is so and what you can do about it.

Fifth, the field of intellectual capital management is young and open to innovation. You therefore have the opportunity as a well-informed business-person to make important contributions both to your enterprise and to this new field. These notes will provide you with a useful frame of reference and will point you to some of the available resources that will help you to make a significant contribution in intellectual capital management, both to your company and to the field generally.

By developing and applying the information I am about to disclose, I have helped improve various companies' long-term operating results by many hundreds of millions of dollars over the years. This is the scope of the benefit that you can provide to your enterprise through implementation of the suggestions and thinking offered in this little book.

Would you like to improve the value of your company by hundreds of millions or billions of dollars? These notes contain a approach for how to do that.

Finally, I keep using the term "intellectual capital." What do I mean by this? Why is this term useful? Why is it preferable to the term, "intellectual property?" Please read on to explore the answers to these questions.

Chapter Two:
Intellectual Capital

The information revolution has changed people's perception of wealth. We originally said that land was wealth. Then we thought it was industrial production. Now we realize it's intellectual capital. The market is showing us that intellectual capital is far more important than money. This is a major change in the way the world works. The same thing that happened to the farmers in the Industrial Revolution is now happening to people in industry as we move into the information age.

—**Walter Wriston:** Interview with Thomas A. Bass—
"The Future of Money," *www.wired.com* (October 1, 1996)

A Very Short Story: James Clerk Maxwell was born in Edinburgh on June 13, 1831. He was educated at the University of Edinburgh and University of Cambridge. He was a professor and researcher throughout his short life and loved Scottish poetry, publishing a volume of his own in 1882. His field was mathematics and physics. Before him, electricity, magnetism, and light were considered separate and distinct from one another. After his publication in 1865 of *A Dynamical Theory of the Electromagnetic Field*, these three forces were regarded as different manifestations of the same phenomenon. All three forms of energy were then understood as fields that travel though space as waves moving at the speed of light. Albert Einstein is reported to have said of Maxwell's work that it was the "most profound and the most fruitful that physics has experienced since the time of Newton."

The moral of this story? Perhaps it is this: the metaphysical world of company intellectual capital may imitate the physical world of electromagnetic energy, uniting human capital, relationship capital, and structural capital in a complex, multi-faceted phenomenon inviting study by conscientious business-people in the same way that electromagnetism invites study by conscientious physicists.

So, what is intellectual capital, and how is it different from intellectual property? Below is a definition of intellectual capital that is meant to be non-controversial and non-innovative. It emphasizes the business and financial nature of a firm's intellectual assets, rather than the legal protections available for those assets and rather than cataloging the various kinds of documents that may represent or legally secure some of those assets. The theory here is that an understanding of intellectual capital ought to clarify rather than confuse—clarify the business nature of the asset class rather than the possible legal protections available for those assets. And it should be a workable definition among the main constituency of its users: business-people. This understanding has been in use now for many years and does not originate with me.

Here it is:

- Intellectual capital refers to the intangible value of a business found in that business's:
  - Human Capital—the professional and tacit knowledge and skill of its people (sometimes referred to as know-how)
  - Relationship Capital—business, financial, regulatory, legislative, civic, charitable, and research relationships (for example) with others such as customers, suppliers, co-development partners, financial institutions, strategic partners, investors, consortium partners, trade associations, standards development organizations, joint venture partners, universities, legislative bodies, politicians, and government agencies, for example, along with the company's reputation or brand
  - Structural Capital—all the other intellectual intangibles that remain, both documented and undocumented, that members of the company consider to be proprietary, beneficial, and/or qualifying and differentiating. For example, structural capital will typically be made up of the following overlapping categories of intellectual assets:
    - » Business models and strategies and their implementing business processes
    - » Innovation-oriented and operational business processes and their implementing infrastructure
    - » Business processes concerning the recruitment and retention of key human capital
    - » Business processes concerning the management of the company's relationship capital
    - » Products and services design/formulation information
    - » Differentiating manufacturing equipment and process design

» Differentiating test equipment and process design
» Experimentation, development, and test results
» Inventions, innovations, and technology
» Financial information
» Customized enterprise operating and reporting software systems
» Analytical and developmental results and tools
» Culture: the undocumented way a company does things and makes decisions, what it values and respects, how it informally differentiates itself in the minds of its employees from other enterprises in its market space, and its guiding priorities and principles
» Intangible products and services (such as software, information, creative works, and privileged access services)
» All other information related to the company, its plans (including strategic and operating plans), and its operations that members of the company consider proprietary

Intellectual capital is the sum of everything everybody in a company knows and has created and is capable of creating that gives it a competitive edge. It is the intellectual asset base typically not listed on a company's balance sheet.

Many people refer to the firm's various types of intellectual assets—such as those categories listed above—with the term "intellectual property." The difficulty with this term is that in its common usage it refers specifically to the bodies of law that may be used to provide legal protections for some intellectual capital assets. The typical short list of these bodies of law is the following: patent law, copyright law, trademark law, and trade secret law.

When many business-people try to think about managing the intellectual capital of the enterprise, it's actually a bit confusing to have to think first about the strength and effectiveness of the legal protections rather than the capitals and the specific assets within the capitals themselves. As often happens, the lawyers cannot with certainty tell us what the strength or effectiveness of the law might be in various countries in which one is doing business. In addition, there are some countries that don't have any trade secret law. Many countries do not have financially adequate remedies available to companies that experience violations of their intellectual property rights and contractual agreements. So, to throw the emphasis in thinking about managing a company's intellectual capital on possible legal protections may be a distraction for many business-people.

Often, an enterprise's ability to compete effectively will depend on a time advantage provided by that firm's uniquely qualifying intellectual capital. This temporal way of understanding the advantage of one's intellectual assets prevents one from relying too heavily on a legal system that may not deliver reliable benefits. And it provides a level of realism in one's thinking about managing one's intellectual capital.

A corollary to a significant time advantage is a significant investment advantage. Some firms have so deep and long an investment history and so deep a pool of human capital and relationship capital in a particular field, as a result of a long history of investments and the conduct of business in a particular area, that it may not make financial sense for another, less-well-advantaged company to try to compete. In other words, an emergent competitor may not have a path to profitability, given the amount of money that must be invested to duplicate or surpass the complex and developmentally expensive intellectual capital of the incumbent firm.

Along side this investment advantage is a company's business partner affinity—its relationship capital. A company that has worked well with a business partner over many years or decades at both the executive level and the lower business and technical levels, can often effectively exclude a potential competitor or can significantly reduce the potential competitor's probability of success in breaking this relationship bond.

In addition, an enterprise's ability to compete effectively can depend on a unique combination of capabilities. Said another way, some companies are unusually successful, not so much because of a time advantage or amount of investment but rather because of their unique store of intellectual capital and other advantages, which others—even given sufficient time and money—are unlikely to duplicate. An example here is Rockwell Collins, which had more than fifty percent of the military Global Positioning System (GPS) receiver market for decades. Its combination of an early and substantial lead in winning key, early government development contracts, expertise in designing hybrid analog and digital chips and systems, deep understanding of military-grade wireless communication protocols, security, and encryption, the excellence of its manufacturing and electronics packaging capability, the stability and professional knowledge and skill of its employees in these areas, its low human capital costs because of its location in Iowa, and its deep relationships with its Department of Defense customers together gave it an overwhelming set of advantages that others found very difficult to equal.

Again, the emphasis here is not on legal protections. In fact, in many unusually successful companies, legal protections rightly occupy little attention of the business-people who run such companies, because the protections they offer are often indeterminate and potentially trivial in comparison with the advantages offered by intellectual capital that may not depend directly on legal protections.

Another example of this unique combination of capabilities—or unique combination of intellectual capital bundles—is Vanguard. The combination of this company's intellectual capital bundles—and its being early to the market with these capabilities—have made it unusually successful in retail investing: business model (customer-owned, versus investor-owned), the charisma and credibility of its former CEO—Jack Bogle—and his personal contribution to the company's brand over many decades, the company's index-oriented investing approach, and the low cost of the company's investment services (enabled by the company's business model and investing approach). Other companies have attempted to imitate Vanguard in some respects, but have struggled to compete with Vanguard's growth rate, market share, low cost, and client satisfaction performance.

Additionally, the superior value of a company's human capital—its professional knowledge and skill, whether tacit or not—can be the driving force of its success. I cannot identify how many situations in which the extraordinary contribution of unique human capital to investment decisions, to culture, to innovation in business processes and business models, to technical solutions, and to relationships and relationship management is at the heart of the matter. And the extraordinary contribution of human capital (in the form of know-how) in transactions can be central to the value of the licensed intellectual capital. In these circumstances, the absence of the critical human capital would very often mean the absence of a transaction—the absence of the real value in the transaction.

Finally, there is the company's business model. Many successful companies innovate the business models that they will develop and deploy, upending the value proposition for products and services in a particular market. Or their innovative business models will create new markets. And when the development and deployment of such new business models is coupled with speed and excellent execution, resulting in early and significant acquisition of market share, competitors will have difficulty catching up.

The Vanguard example above is also a good illustration of the power of an innovative business model. Another is Airbnb. By enabling apartment renters and owners and detached-home owners to become entrepreneurs, Airbnb restructured the short-term room-rental and home-rental market and enabled customers to rent housing that is often more comfortable and at rates that are more competitive than the traditional hotel industry was offering in many markets. Business travelers and leisure travelers were rewarded and consequentially made Airbnb a market leader in a very few years. Because Airbnb moved quickly in many markets simultaneously, they stayed ahead of potential copycat competitors and continued to attract the lion's share of the investment dollars available for this business approach.

So, the lesson here is that the enterprise's intellectual capital value is often in areas that are not protected or protectable by intellectual property law.

As business-people invest in the development of intellectual capital, they will often have little idea about the defensibility and value of the legal protections that may or may not be available. Very often, business-people must make investment decisions in the development of intellectual capital with the assumption that the legal protections are potentially insignificant. They must base their value assessment on the assumption that one or more of the six areas of advantage listed above—time, magnitude of the investment, relationship capital, unique mix of intellectual capital assets, unique human capital, and innovative business models, along with other better understood business advantages such as overhead structure costs, delivery terms, price, etc.—will provide the real source of differentiation and of future cash flows, rather than specific legal protections.

(Of course, there are important and significant exceptions. The pharmaceutical industry, for example, is notable for its reliance on patents. Without a strong patent, a new molecule cannot get the extraordinary scale of funding that is required for a new drug's development and testing. And without the ability to exclude competitors from practicing the invention that a pharmaceutical patent provides, a company developing a new drug cannot make the financials work. So, this industry obviously does focus quite closely and relentlessly on the strength of critical legal protection—specifically patents. There are other exceptions as well: companies that rely on patent licensing revenue as a major element in their profit expectations, for example.)

(There also are universities, research laboratories, and startups. Such organizations sometimes rightly rely heavily on patents. In the case of some universities and research laboratories—those whose business models include licensing of their technology to others—patents may be a key element in any investor's due diligence, when it considers funding a startup licensee or investing in an operating company agreeing to take a license. With a keen interest in publications, universities are seldom able to offer trade secrets for license and are therefore focused on their patents. In these examples, enterprise leadership should be focused on the strength of the legal protections, since the success of their business models will correctly depend heavily on these protections. And of course, the entertainment industry relies heavily on the strength of copyrights and trademarks. Think of Woody Woodpecker, here, or Mickey Mouse, or the Black Panther, or the Chicago Cubs (well, maybe not so much the Chicago Cubs)).

In many companies (outside of the kinds of enterprises listed in the parentheses above), the business-person wanting to manage the enterprise's intellectual capital assets well actually wants to know specifically what these assets are more than he wants to know what may or may not be the strength of the legal protections available for those assets. Said another way, intellectual capital is not the legal protections that may or may not effectively protect it; rather, these structural, relationship, and human capital assets are know-how, information of various kinds, software, designs, culture, business models, etc. Therefore, the benefit of using the term "intellectual capital" is that it does not provide the misdirection of the term "intellectual property." It more cleanly points to what the intangible assets in fact are. And the term suggests the essential financial nature of these assets, which is a benefit to business-people, who are educated to manage business and financial assets, not legal protection mechanisms.

The term "intellectual capital" includes areas of intangibles that are definitely not covered by intellectual property law: human capital and relationship capital. And even within the area of structural capital, there are areas that intellectual property law cannot help much with: culture and business models. These are critical areas for any operating company. Good management of the intangibles in these areas is critical to the success of the enterprise, and it is useful to develop and apply business management policy and process to all forms of the company's intellectual assets. The term "intellectual capital" brings three critical areas of a company's intangibles (human capital, relationship capital, and structural capital) under one management framework.

Very often, when people use the term "intellectual property," they do not even consider the company's human capital, relationship capital, business models, culture, the company's unique software (both software in the company's operating infrastructure and software tools and frameworks, as well as software products), and the company's information and access-based services. In other words, even within the area of structural capital, people often exclude key intangible assets from their thinking when they try to reason about and manage the company's "intellectual property" store.

Finally, business-people generally think that "intellectual property" is the field in which the lawyers work, along with a few misguided business-people who find the licensing of intangibles interesting. This is suboptimal. The management of an enterprise's intellectual capital should be the main focus of enterprise business management, and it often isn't. Or these assets—because they are not well understood—are therefore often managed sub-optimally.

We must do something different. And we must signal that we are doing something different by changing our vocabulary so that it is more directly relevant to the way of thinking of business-people. Specialists in change management affirm that a change in vocabulary can help reorient the thinking of the enterprise, making the desired change easier to bring about. And besides, as I have implied above, much of a company's valuable intellectual capital is either not protected or not protectable under most countries' intellectual property law. And if it is "protectable" under a country's intellectual property law, the remedies for theft and misuse are often underwhelming.

Suggesting or implying that most valuable intellectual capital is financially secured in some way by most countries' intellectual property law is misdirection. It is confusing, even to the people who think of themselves as specialists in the field of intellectual property. (I know this from personal experience. I cannot tell you how many confusing conversations I have had with lawyers and business-people about the possible effectiveness and value of specific investments in intellectual capital creation and development—confusing because we will often go down the rabbit hole of speculating about what the effectiveness of the legal protections may or may not be at some difficult-to-identify point and place in the future.) And of course, these confusing conversations drive the business-people right round the bend: business-people tell me that such discussions seem to them to be a complete waste of time. (And in more than a few cases in my experience, they were!)

Now, let us return to our definition of intellectual capital. For the record, key legal protections that may or may not be available for the human capital component of a company's intellectual capital may be contract law relating to employment agreements and non-compete agreements, as well as labor and employment law.

Key legal protections that may or may not be available for the relationship capital component of a company's intellectual capital may involve contract law and intellectual property law—specifically trademark law.

Key legal protections that may or may not be available for the structural capital component of a company's intellectual capital may be intellectual property law—patent, copyright, and trade secret law—as well as contract law.

Publications on the subject of "intellectual capital" first flourished in the 1990s and the early 2000s, as academics and business practitioners observed a pivot in the United States and elsewhere from an industrial economy to an information and knowledge economy. A few academics continue to work and write in the field of intellectual capital, but in the world of business books and articles focused on an audience of business practitioners, the rate of new publication and new thinking on the subject has slowed.

It is hard to explain this slowing of new ideas and material. Perhaps the subject is simply too large and amorphous to write about concisely or usefully. Perhaps the discipline is too immature. Perhaps business practitioners and their consultants—who are the source of much popular and practical business literature—find it more useful to focus on other topics (or selected sub-topics), rather than on so broad and diverse a field. Perhaps the audience for such books is too small. Perhaps the confusion introduced by inconsistent and misleading vocabulary has impeded clear thinking in this area. Perhaps the academic community has not focused its attention on research, information, and insights that really matter to business-people.

This is speculation. I simply have no idea why new publication and new thinking in the field of practitioner-oriented intellectual capital management has slowed.

All of that being said, and now that we have a definition, of sorts, where to go from here? As a practitioner or possible practitioner, you are probably wondering what the definition means: What are some illustrative examples?

As I say, my background is in the aerospace and defense industry; so, my categories above may reflect that. Within these categories, there are many documentary and non-documentary examples. But perhaps there is another time and place for that. I don't want to bog us down here. (Once it issues, please see the LES Intellectual Assets in the Boardroom Standard for many examples of documentary intellectual capital assets. There is more on intellectual capital management standards and intellectual capital assets in Chapter 7: Standards.)

Suffice it to say that the categories above and any examples are important because most business-people in most companies relate to categories of intellectual property law, contract law, and other forms of law like NASCAR drivers relate to amoeba. They don't.

To manage intellectual capital well, most business people need to have in mind what it actually is—what the assets actually are—and less what the legal protections may or may not be and how effective or ineffective they may or may not be. Notionally, we'd like to know what the relative value is of one bundle of intellectual capital rights versus another. And we'd like to know what the investments are in a particular area of intellectual capital and what the payoff or return on those investments is or should be.

We would like to know what intellectual capital is differentiating versus table stakes. And on the subject of intellectual capital that is viewed as table stakes, we'd like to know how difficult an insurgent—a new entrant into the market—would find duplicating that particular class of intellectual capital.

We would like to know how well we are managing our intellectual capital—whether we are using best practices or not. We'd like to know what those best practices are.

And we'd like to know much, much more.

We cannot reason about any of this, if we don't have in mind what the key areas of intellectual capital are—and what the key intellectual capital assets are—for our enterprise.

Legal protections can be important, but they are not central to many of the questions and processes business-people use to manage most intellectual capital in many companies, indeed in many industries. Therefore, while the lawyers and the specialists in intellectual capital management should definitely pay a great deal of attention to ensuring that reasonable legal protections are secured, this work should generally not be the focus of the business-people. Setting aside the parenthetical exceptions above (and of course, the list above is not exhaustive), the legal protection work should be a "back office" function provided by the lawyers and intellectual capital management experts, with support, of course, from the inventors and developers of the intellectual capital in question.

Before we get started, one more point. In these notes I intend to pay greater attention to what companies might do to manage their structural capital well. Many companies today put significant resources into managing their human capital and relationship capital, and there are substantial bodies of literature in both areas. With the management of structural capital—e.g. proprietary information, tools, technology, customized company operating system software, software tools, and intangible products and services (such as software and information services)—there are substantial resources involved, but there is less in the way of literature and systematic management theory. This is the low-hanging fruit mentioned in the Preface.

Since a significant locus of structural capital management happens in the context of the negotiation and management of intellectual capital rights with one's business partners (e.g. customers, suppliers, co-development partners, and government agencies), particularly in business-to-business enterprises, relationship capital is very much involved. In other words, in managing the relationships with one's business partners, one simultaneously needs to manage the structural capital and the human capital (know-how) matters involved in these relationships. The three sorts of intellectual capital are intertwined.

So while I will focus on structural capital throughout this discussion, please keep in mind that its management is integral with the management of the company's business relationships and the management of its human capital's know-how contributions to business partner collaborations and interactions. As the management of a company's intellectual capital evolves, so should the management of one's relationship capital and one's human capital involved in collaborative relationships.

An important side note: many transactions won't have much value without the know-how provided by specific people. So licensing of structural capital often won't make much sense or be worth much without the licensing of the know-how provided by the human capital, which will be required to activate the documented (or sometimes substantially undocumented) structural capital. Further, the human capital in collaborative work with other companies has a tendency to put know-how contributions into the hands of the other party without appropriate reference back to the original intellectual capital rights agreement. This (along with the problem of undocumented intellectual capital contributions of the parties, as the work evolves) can be a significant risk to the companies' intellectual capital rights, at the end of the day.

The professional knowledge and skill of many actors in the company will need to be enhanced to achieve better financial performance at the product, business unit, and corporate levels. One cannot effect enterprise-wide changes without improving the know-how of the members of the firm. And one certainly cannot achieve better financial outcomes without changing the nature and quality of the way one manages relationships with one's business partners, where structural capital and human capital are involved. In other words, one must move beyond bluff and bluster discussions about intellectual capital rights to reasoned value-based discussions about such rights.

Before we move on, perhaps it would be useful to discuss the difficulty of changing terminology, changing the subject of one's focus, changing one's understanding of what one is doing, and changing one's notional identity as someone who manages intellectual capital.

Some lawyers don't like this term, because it diminishes their organizational power and control. If we define the bundles of assets we are interested in as something that is not legal in nature, but rather something else—intellectual capital—we diminish the lawyers' control over the dialog and management decisions related to these assets. If we define intellectual assets as financial rather than legal assets, we diminish the lawyers' ability to exert control over the management of intellectual capital within the company and within the field of intellectual capital management generally.

I have had many conversations with lawyers about this. Many are fine with this approach, seeing it as part of a healthy evolution in the understanding and competencies of the business-people in companies. But a few would want to nix my ability to teach and to coach and to consult on this topic on the premise that I am trying to guide people in legal matters. Of course, I'm not. I'm trying to teach, coach, and consult on intellectual capital matters—intangible financial matters, not legal matters. I'm trying to teach others how to manage intellectual capital better.

Terminology, then, is a big deal. Changing the way we talk about intellectual assets from "intellectual property" to "intellectual capital" is a big deal. It's not just a change in the lingo. It represents a change in what we're talking about, what we are doing, the universe in which we live and work, and who we are—what sort of professionals we are. In this case, it represents a broadening in what the intellectual assets management profession actually is and what the concerns of the profession are, what the activities of the profession are, and who the members of the profession are. All of this is critical, if we are to help companies manage intellectual capital—particularly structural capital and know-how—better. We need a vocabulary that speaks to the business-people and that they can use to discuss business issues, rather than legal issues.

(A bit more on the terminology: I've defined intellectual capital above. It includes both documentary intellectual capital—e.g., contracts, software documentation, product test data, product design information, and so forth—along with non-documentary intellectual capital, such as know-how, tacit knowledge, personal relationships, culture, business models, etc. In this short book, I refer to "intellectual capital assets" and "intellectual assets" and "intangible assets" from time to time, and by those terms, I'm referring to all sorts of "instances" of intellectual capital, whether structural capital, human capital, and relationship capital, whether documentary or non-documentary. Sometimes I may inadvertently use the term "non-tangible assets" and by it I mean the same thing.)

(I apologize if there are inconsistencies and potential confusions between the vocabulary I advance here and the traditional accounting vocabulary. I'm an imperfect human being, and these are merely a set of notes, after all. They're not meant to be complete or finished or definitive in any way. They're meant as an invitation to improvement and revision by everyone who has an interest. They are meant to stimulate further work and thinking and writing and to be superseded.)

Most professionals in most companies manage intellectual capital directly or indirectly. Very few business-people who are involved with managing intellectual capital would say they are licensing professionals or commercialization professionals or business development professionals. Most of them could not tell you the difference between intellectual property and intellectual capital. They are merely managing products, programs, program pursuits, R&D projects, infrastructure development projects, tool development projects, new business model development, pricing, customers, suppliers, and their company's investment decisions. And this is a problem—not understanding a key aspect of what one is doing, as a business-person. Not having a vocabulary that is suited to talking about and reasoning about an important aspect of what one is doing.

Because if we don't have an effective vocabulary to talk about and write about what we are doing, we are likely going to have a difficult time focusing on how to do what we are doing better.

So where to next? I'd like to suggest a set of questions for you to consider. If after considering these questions, you conclude that your company is in fine shape, you probably shouldn't read any further, because it would likely be a waste of your time. But if after reading the questions and probing around a bit in your company, you think there may be some room for improvement in how intellectual capital is being managed, continued reading may be in order.

Chapter Three:

Questions

How can someone make a relatively quick and systematic assessment of the company's basic capabilities in intellectual capital management? Here below are several key questions one might consider. (There are certainly others one might ask, but I'm trying to keep this short and basic.)

1. Is there a formal company policy regarding pricing intellectual capital rights (whether selling rights or buying rights) that: (1) requires a valuation of those rights formulated by an expert in the valuation of intellectual capital rights, (2) uses valuation of those rights when licensing out to set the delegation of authority for pricing those rights, rather than the price of those rights, and (3) accounts for all meaningful kinds of intellectual capital rights (e.g. technology, business processes, intangible products and services, know-how, etc.)?

2. Are there holistic and effective business processes that enable the company to assess its intellectual capital assets at a granular-enough level that it can develop other effective business processes for protecting sufficiently valuable intellectual capital (and sufficiently protecting valuable intellectual capital) from disclosure (and perhaps licensing) to others? Is the assessment of those valuable assets quantitative, where a quantitative analysis would be a benefit to understanding? Do those business processes to protect valuable company intellectual capital from disclosure include a gate-keeper function and the criterion of "need to know?"

3. Is there a formal business and technical process by which the company's intellectual capital is protected when "at rest?" Does this include effective access control (compartmentalization) and authentication? Does it include adequate encryption?

4. Is it well understood who the intellectual capital valuation experts are and when they need to be engaged?

5. Is there a formal business process by which transactions involving intellectual capital rights are conducted?

6. Is there a formal business process by which one business unit co-ordinates intellectual capital rights licensing or sale with relevant other business units who either "own" or paid for the development of the subject intellectual capital or who otherwise have a business interest in the subject intellectual capital?

7. Is there a formal, effective business and technical process by which company intellectual capital is supplied to others, including adequate information security and compartmentalization?

8. Is there a formal business and technical process by which the company protects business partners' intellectual capital, including access control (compartmentalization), authentication, and encryption?

9. Is there a formal business process by which the company "trues up" objectives, terms, intellectual capital rights, and conveyances in on-going joint development programs?

10. Do the procurement and contracts organizations treat business process protection requirements concerning company intellectual capital—inside the company's business partners—as seriously and thoroughly as the company treats the protection of its own and others' intellectual capital? Are these requirements adequate?

11. Is there a formal business process by which transfer pricing for intellectual capital rights is determined and managed? Is it based on input from intellectual capital rights valuation experts?

12. Are the above business processes published, taught, communicated, reinforced, monitored, and assessed regularly to ensure that they are effective?

13. Are escapes tracked and lessons learned from them worked into updates to the above business processes and the teaching and communication of those processes?

14. Do you have an organizational construct by which these questions can be asked and answered effectively?

If after reading and considering these questions and after probing your company's business processes, you have concluded that there is room for improvement, then I would propose that you read on. Otherwise, stop.

Today, companies expect business-people—program managers, product line managers, brand managers, business developers, customer account managers, business relationship managers, technology development leaders, product developers, supply chain managers, pricing professionals, and others—to know how to manage intellectual capital well. Some people in some companies don't. (Maybe many people in some companies don't.)

My belief is that some (perhaps many) companies need an expert or perhaps a cadre of experts in the area of intellectual capital transactions and management to lead the company's practice in the important areas referred to above. The next chapter discusses what such an expert or cadre of experts might do to improve the company's intellectual capital management practice and ultimately its financial performance.

Chapter Four:
What Might a Cadre of
Intellectual Capital Management Experts Do?

If a man empties his purse into his head, no man can take it from him.
An investment in knowledge pays the best interest.

—**Benjamin Franklin:** *The Way to Wealth*

Intangible capital takes various forms. It can be protected by legal rights (often termed intellectual property), such as patents and trademarks, or it can be in an unprotected, know-how state. It can be embedded in durable products such as software operating machine tools, or it can stand alone—for example, as brands. Intangible capital is increasingly present in the form of organizational assets—the unique organizational and managerial designs of business enterprises. Here, too, the ability to leverage organizational capital to achieve efficiencies and create value far exceeds the value creation ability of physical assets.

—**Baruch Lev:** *Intangibles*

A Very Short Story: Lillian Moller Gilbreth was born Lillian Evelyn Moller on May 24, 1878, in Oakland, California. She graduated from the University of California at Berkeley with a major in English in 1900, and she graduated from the same university with a master's degree in English in 1902. She married Frank Bunker Gilbreth in 1904, a man who had not attended college at all and was involved in building construction, bricklaying to begin with. There he discovered his true calling when he developed ways to make bricklaying faster and easier for the worker. In this work—work to redesign how work in enterprises is performed, to achieve higher levels of efficiency and worker safety and well-being—he began to collaborate with his new wife, and the two of them founded their consulting firm, Gilbreth, Inc. Lillian finished her work on her PhD at the University of California at Berkeley, including her dissertation, by 1911, but because she did not meet the residency requirements, she was not awarded the degree. The title of the dissertation was *The Psychology of Management: The Function of the Mind in Determining, Teaching, and Install-ing Methods of Least Waste*, which was published in 1914. After relocating with her husband and large family from New York to Providence, Rhode Island, she enrolled in Brown University. There, she was finally awarded a PhD in 1915, in applied psychology. While her husband made substantial contributions to the field that today is called industrial engineering, she laid the foundation for the field that is now called industrial and organizational psychology. They worked together in their consulting firm until her husband's death in 1924, and she carried on the work of the firm through mid-century. She was a prolific inventor, and many aspects of the modern home found their origin in her work. Ms. Gilbreth was a popular speaker at business and industry gatherings at many prestigious colleges and universities. In 1935, she became a professor of management at Purdue's School of Mechanical Engineering. She was promoted to full professor there in 1940 and established and supervised a time-and-motion study laboratory at Purdue's School of Industrial Engineering. She was best known as a pioneer in the field of management theory, winning many awards and honorary degrees throughout her long and fruitful career. A polymath, if there ever was one. A cross-disciplinary hero and a co-founder of the field of systematic business management.

The moral of this story? Perhaps it is this: thought leadership in the field of business management can come from anywhere, even from bricklayers and English majors. The Gilbreths should inspire all of us to new levels of understanding of how to manage companies and their assets better, to create increased value for customers, investors, employees, supply chain partners, and communities.

Introduction

So where are we going, here? Top level, we are headed toward a somewhat modified operational concept of the firm, with a new group of experts in intellectual capital management leading the organization's work in this area. Through the development of policies, processes, procedures, instructions, tools, education, audits, messaging, metrics and reporting, communication, standards, negotiation best practices, and business consulting in a variety of areas (valuation, strategy, and business models, for example) in intellectual capital management, such a group can lead the development of a new set of capabilities and ways of doing business for the company. Such a group can teach the company how to manage intellectual capital better and can stimulate and equip the people in the company's business units to manage intellectual capital better.

At the heart of any concept of enterprise intellectual capital management is the value of the enterprise's intellectual capital store and its capacity for increasing that store. In other words, to manage intellectual capital, we ought to have a sense of what the stakes are for managing it well or managing it poorly. We ought somehow to get a handle on what the associated cash flows are that may be optimized or sub-optimized and what the impact to the business could be by agreeing to licensing arrangements (both in and out) of various kinds. We'd like to be able to associate our investments in intellectual capital with the equity value of the company. When investing in intellectual capital, we'd like to know the financial payoff. By choosing not to invest, we'd like to know the financial harm. And where there is considerable uncertainty, we'd like to have an assessment of the likely range of uncertainty and the assumptions used in the analysis.

Not all intellectual capital is created equal. Some is deserving of much greater investment than others, and some is deserving of much greater care—through legal, physical, technical (information technology (IT)), human resources, and business process means—than others. Some should be commercialized quickly and some slowly. Some needs to be combined with another company's products or services or intellectual capital to realize its full value potential, and other intellectual capital is best developed to maturity in isolation before it sees the light of day.

Think of an enterprise's store of intellectual capital as similar to the Mississippi River watershed. The value of this watershed can be assessed as its financial benefit in recreational services. Its value can also be assessed as a means of shipping goods inexpensively up and down its course and up and down the course of its major tributaries. The value of the water it provides for supporting people, agriculture, and industry as against the absence of it could be assessed. In other words, what if the Mississippi watershed were a desert?

There are many ways of assessing the value of and extracting value from the various types of intellectual capital assets a company will create, and there are various ways of protecting against misuse and therefore preserving the value of a company's intellectual capital. Nearly everyone in a company is involved in managing a company's intellectual capital, but a cadre of business experts in intellectual capital valuation, in intellectual capital rights deal-making, in the development of business strategies that are keyed to optimizing the value of a company's intellectual capital, and in development and management of policies, processes, and tools by which intellectual capital is managed can make a big difference.

Like a human resources organization, such a group can provide the education, tools, and guidance by which the organization improves the management of its intellectual capital—and thus its financial performance. And such a group—as with human resources—will want to work closely with specialist lawyers to make sure the legal issues related to intellectual capital management are well attended to.

The following sections touch on some of the areas in the enterprise in which such a cadre of business-people can add value and can help lead the way.

Enterprise Business Models

One of the critical kinds of enterprise intellectual capital is the enterprise's collection of business models, because these business models have everything to do with the financial success the enterprise is able to achieve. The enterprise's business models, all taken together, constitute the enterprise's most visible way of doing business, and this way of doing business allows the enterprise to turn its investment capital into intellectual capital and its intellectual capital into cash flows coming from products and services.

A significant element of an enterprise business model is what position the enterprise chooses or is chosen to occupy in either existing or new markets and in either existing or new value chains and value networks. For example, consider Qualcomm, a company with which I had a little experience in the early to mid-1990s. At that time, it was a service provider to the trucking industry, providing satellite-based two-way messaging and geolocation services.

Qualcomm was started by two very bright and energetic communications technologists—former college professors—and entrepreneurs (Irwin Jacobs and Andrew Viterbi), along with several others. The wireless technology on which they based their truck location and messaging business was direct sequence spread spectrum, a technology devised for secure wireless communication shortly after World War II, by an inventor at ITT—Lou Rogoff.

Turns out, direct sequence spread spectrum technology is also very advantageous for achieving wireless communication efficiency, by enabling much more information to be packed into a segment of spectrum than other alternatives. The leaders at Qualcomm decided to advocate the use of direct sequence as the basis for an alternative digital cellular communications standard. They surprised many in the industry and were successful.

Then they proceeded to change the structure of the value chain in cellular telephony, putting innovation at the heart of the value proposition—spectrum efficiency, specifically, and cellular communication technical standards—and displacing incumbents who had superior manufacturing capability, relatively inexpensive access to cash, and market channel dominance. A key aspect of their value was in their highly innovative engineering team and in their ability to translate this team's technical know-how rapidly into technical innovations, product implementations, patents, and, of course, standards.

The rapidity of their innovations, the excellence of their implementations and their patents, their audacity in their willingness to go a different direction in communication technology than the industry was taking at the time, the persuasiveness of their technical arguments in the technical standards committees, and the strength of their partnership strategies with operators (both international and domestic) gave them their breakthrough. They upended the value chain among the existing players, delivering significant value to operators and subscribers, and developing significant market power as a chip supplier and patent licensor, versus their handset and wireless infrastructure customers.

It wasn't just technology innovation and the resulting patents that made the difference for Qualcomm, even though they have been essential. Through their human capital, relationship capital, and other structural capital core competencies, they were able to redefine an industry, making a place for themselves at the center of that industry. They took one set of core competencies that they had developed in the vehicle two-way messaging and tracking business and deployed them in an entirely different way in a very different market.

Qualcomm is a good example of what successful business model and value chain innovation looks like. Business processes that enable companies like Qualcomm to redeploy their core competencies (intellectual capital) from application to application and market to market with reduced risk and enhanced payoff are key. Developing, maintaining, measuring, and improving such business processes is an important set of intellectual capital management activities in companies today.

Of course, we have many other excellent examples of companies that have innovated industry business models and by doing so have achieved stunning financial performance, companies such as Microsoft, Google, Amazon, and Facebook.

Licensing of intellectual capital in its many forms can be a versatile added dimension to the construction of unique or innovative business models. For example, there are tens of billions of dollars per year exchanged in licenses to patents that read on technical standards. Many companies significantly augment their profit performance through patent licensing keyed to technical standards, and I have mentioned one of them above: Qualcomm. There are quite a few others.

The point here is that there are many approaches to business model innovation, and one of them is intellectual capital licensing, whether that comes in the form of patent licensing, trademark licensing (think of Disney here), movie and music rights licensing, network access licensing (wireless cellular services subscriptions or cable services subscriptions), software licensing (often through subscriptions), information services licensing (often through subscriptions), hosting services licensing (infrastructure access subscription services), etc.

When intellectual capital is licensed—specifically when a bundle of technology rights is licensed—a differentiating element of the bundle may be in the know-how (the human capital) provided, along with an enabled business model innovation. In other words, in the world of technology licensing, while there may be some intellectual property (e.g., patents, copyrights, trademarks, and trade secrets) that is part of the bundle, what comes along as one of the more valuable elements, often invisibly, are the activating know-how of the inventors and practitioners and the business model innovation that is enabled by the intellectual capital bundle. Often in such cases, the business model innovation itself must be taught, in addition to the technological know-how, because the prospective licensee may not understand the innovation well enough to envision its optimal deployment in the marketplace.

Finally, there are well understood financial modelling techniques that the intellectual capital management professional can employ to understand the value of deploying a company's intellectual capital in various business model configurations. Net present value analysis, along with a disciplined approach to selecting the right discount rate to reflect a firm's cost of capital and the particular technical and business risks, is fundamental. And so is accounting for uncertainty through a range-of-results analysis.

But core business model innovation is just one locus of intellectual capital management. What about supply chain?

Business Partner Risk

Most sizable companies have an international supply chain and international customers, and they must share valuable intellectual capital rights with these business partners, as well as international government agencies of various kinds. Many international business partner networks extend into emerging markets. The issue with business partners in emerging market countries is often either that the intellectual property law and the contract law are immature or that the application of these legal regimes is not dependable. And by dependable, I mean that violation of a company's intellectual capital rights in such countries may not typically result in a reasonable remedy—injunctive relief and/or reasonable damages.

In this context—like the business model context—the ability to calculate and understand the dollars and cents value of the intellectual capital can be critical, either prior to disclosure or post-disclosure, when a company's cash flows have been damaged by the misusing party. And it can be important prior to disclosure to understand the business partner's business processes around protecting third party intellectual capital to assess the risk associated with exposing the intellectual capital in question to the supplier, customer, government authority, or co-development partner in question.

All of this entails a critical set of analyses and business processes that are focused on the decision to expose a company's intellectual capital to a particular business partner or government authority in a particular country. Without a value-based understanding of the intellectual capital in such a circumstance, it is difficult to make informed business decisions. And without an informed understanding of what is effective in the custodianship of third-party intellectual capital, one cannot competently frame up requirements for a business partner's or government agency's custodianship of a company's intellectual capital.

The assessment of risk can benefit from a quantitative understanding of the strength of countries' laws and the certainty of dependable remedies in the case of intellectual capital theft and misuse. At this writing, there are two indexes that can help assess this risk, and they are typically updated every year. The first is the "International Property Rights Index." As its name implies, it attempts to assess the strength of the real property and intellectual property protection regimes in countries throughout the world. It is published by the Property Rights Alliance, an advocacy group and think tank in Washington, D.C. The second is the "International Intellectual Property Index," published by the Global Innovation Policy Center of the U.S. Chamber of Commerce.

Of the two publications, the first covers more countries, while the latter seems more thorough in the assessment of the various dimensions of a country's intellectual capital protection regime. Both are available online.

What makes careful attention to this area of intellectual capital management so important is the fact that a huge percentage of intellectual capital theft and misappropriation occurs through a company's business partners and government agencies. I've seen estimates in various publications of 50 percent and more. That is, 50 percent of all theft and misuse of Western companies' valuable intellectual capital happens when intellectual capital thieves reach into those companies' business partners and relevant government agencies and make a copy of the company's intellectual capital.

The damage done can be devastating, in part because proving theft of intellectual capital in a court can be quite difficult—particularly proprietary information—and in part because proving the full extent of the economic damages in a court can be even more difficult. More important than these considerations, often a company won't even know that the theft has taken place—only that its economic success is significantly diminished by a surprisingly innovative and effective competitor.

What this means is that often companies do not monitor others' potential misuse, and they often don't have business partner and government agency requirements in place—with frequent auditing rights—that will provide assurance that the custodian of valuable intellectual capital is in fact implementing effective policies, procedures, education, and control approaches that will protect the company's intellectual capital.

Investment, Innovation, and Commercialization

Another typical locus of intellectual capital value is in a company's business processes involved with the management of research and development investment, innovation, and commercialization of that innovation. In many cases, speed and efficiency are critical to obtaining acceptable or out-performing market penetration rates and acceptable or out-performing returns on the company's research and development (R&D) investments. Obviously, metrics on the performance of the company's investment, innovation, and commercialization (II&C) business process can be critical to a company's performance over time.

At the macro-level, it is possible to assess a company's success in this regard by assessing its ratio of reported operating profit to reported R&D in a given year. But this approach is backward-looking and generic. To achieve proactive and effective intellectual capital management, a company should be forward-looking in its projected return on investment on a project-by-project and business-area-by-business-area basis. Its investment decisions and business process improvements should be guided by a forward-looking financial analysis, with an assessment of intellectual capital value at the heart of such analysis.

An understanding of the value difference in product differentiation enabled by II&C efficiency, market penetration rates, first-mover advantage, channel strategy effectiveness, and so forth can be critical to selecting one path versus another. Methodologically rigorous intellectual capital valuation and financial modeling can be a crucial skill informing business decision-making through the II&C process.

I recall a conversation I had with a management consultant back in the middle 1990s, when Iridium—a spinout from Motorola—was getting ready to launch its first satellites. At that time, cellular networks and cellular access points were proliferating at a dramatic rate, at a much faster rate than the Iridium team had apparently anticipated. The consultant's company was crunching the numbers for Iridium, in order to advise them on subscription pricing for wireless services involving their soon-to-emerge satellite network.

Of course, at that stage, the supposed advantage of the Motorola intellectual capital and its associated value were falling off a cliff. Iridium declared bankruptcy in 1999, shortly after Al Gore—the vice president of the United States at the time—placed the first Iridium call. Lesson learned: intellectual capital rights valuation, financial modeling, and innovation adoption analysis should be done earlier and not only later.

You might ask how one might have been able to assess the intellectual capital value of the critical networking innovations that enabled the Iridium concept, back in the early 1990s, prior to the billions of dollars of investment in manufacturing and launching of the initial 77-satellite network. The answer is that commercialization and diffusion of innovation even at that time was a pretty well-understood phenomenon.

A researcher by the name of Everett Rogers (BS in Agriculture and MS and PhD in Rural Sociology—another polymath) had been publishing information on the diffusion of innovation for decades and had developed a family of curves to describe the process statistically. He accompanied these curves with cultural and psychological characterizations as well. His most famous publication was an often revised and edited book on the topic called, oddly enough, *Diffusion of Innovations*. This groundbreaking book was first published in 1962. Through a statistical analysis of the adoption of hybrid corn throughout the Midwest following World War II, and then through similar analyses on the diffusion of other innovations as the years went by, he developed the well-known diffusion of innovations adoption curve or S-curve.

Subsequently, in the 1990s, Geoffrey Moore (bachelor's and doctorate in Literature—another polymath) published *Crossing the Chasm* and *Inside the Tornado*, both of which popularized Everett Rogers' work and taught Rogers' sigmoid-based innovation adoption curve in a Silicon Valley context.

Such a statistical and financial analysis approach works to describe a successful innovation, but it doesn't do a very good job of describing an unsuccessful one. So, while a sigmoid curve works pretty well on cellular communication, it wouldn't have worked so well on a satellite-based global telephone service. For Iridium to have significantly disrupted the cellular uptake rate, it would have had to provide both a technological and value innovation. Its subscription cost would have had to be cheaper than or at least competitive with cellular, but the operator economics did not work out that way.

Iridium's massive investment in ground-based infrastructure and its satellite network, as well as its financial obligations to its telephone company operating partners around the world, would not allow for pricing that would be competitive with cellular. So, while Motorola had developed a stunning technological innovation, this did not result in a concomitant value innovation for most of the market Iridium wanted to serve. And this was knowable prior to the point when the lion's share of the investments needed to be made. In other words, the cellular S-curve was well-established and predictable by that time. Cellular operator costs and profits and pricing were well-understood. And Iridium's costs, time to market, investment holding period, return on investment requirements, discount rate, and pricing requirements all were knowable within a reasonable uncertainty window.

The upshot (so to speak)? My consultant friend's financial analysis—pessimistic as it was—was received. My friend was thanked and paid for his work. And Iridium continued on its way.

Most potential subscribers served by cellular or soon to be served by cellular were not interested in Iridium's service. It was only through the commitment of the US government and a few other strategic investors that the Iridium capability was maintained. Today governments are responsible for about 25% of Iridium's revenue, while maritime, aviation, and remote users of various kinds (outside of cellular service areas) make up the rest of its customer base. At this writing, Iridium has about a million global subscribers, while cellular operators have about 4.6 billion subscribers.

Now, in 2020, we have a new competition for a satellite-based wireless service: an internet-based suite of services to be offered to a variety of businesses, schools, mobile platforms, and individuals (for example), both within coverage of 5G cellular internet services and wired internet services and outside of such coverages. Starlink and OneWeb are the two most visible contenders to provide such satellite-based services. Time will tell whether the satellite-based business model can survive the buildout of 5G cellular services and whether there is a sufficient value innovation to sustain the celestial economics of such endeavors.

As to the development of metrics related to the speed and efficiency of moving innovation into products and services, there are many ways to do this. The important thing here is to do it, and to do so on a project-by-project and business-area-by-business-area basis. As people in the engineering, program management, product development, business development, and strategy functions learn, metrics and performance should improve.

There's nothing more destructive of investment value and intellectual capital value than for business leadership to dither in its investment decision-making or engineering leadership to dither in its innovation and development work or marketing leadership to dither in taking the innovative product or service to market. Treading water in any of these critical areas usually means allowing competitors to catch up, and that often means the erosion of intellectual capital value. Intellectual capital innovations that deliver incremental value do not have an infinite shelf life.

Often, one of the most fundamental and effective intellectual capital protection schemes involves time—the temporal lead one has on one's competitors.

Finally, early stage technology innovation is often difficult to model. Many early stage innovations that seem quite remarkable go nowhere. This is because they do not provide substantial value enhancement over and above the technology and business solutions that are in place or that are predictable improvements on what is in place. At an early stage, it may not be clear whether the innovation, once commercialized, will in fact provide that superior value proposition. But as development proceeds and commercialization costs and the required pricing of the products and services, along with the required return on investment, begin to clarify, the relative value proposition and financial benefit can be estimated.

Supply Chain Licensing

Another locus of realized (or lost) intellectual capital value within companies is within their intellectual capital rights transaction processes that take place in the normal course of their product and service businesses. Some industries are highly collaborative, sharing intellectual capital rights with suppliers, customers, co-development partners, government agencies, and competitors. In addition to the buying and selling context, intellectual capital knowledge is also shared in a pre-transaction or ex-transaction sense through collaboration on technical and business process standards. For example, Qualcomm is very active in a number of technical standards committees and subsequently expects to license its patents that read on some of these standards.

But outside of standards essential patent licensing, trademark licensing, and commercialization licensing (e.g., by universities to entrepreneurs), the fact is that in many business-to-business transactions of intellectual capital rights, no value calculation is done, because the transaction is done by people who have little-to-no knowledge of intellectual capital rights valuation. Rights are often ceded in the context of a business relationship that is characterized by an exchange of favors and concessions of various kinds, along with the sale of goods and services. In other words, many business-people doing intellectual capital rights transactions in the course of their normal business view intellectual capital licensing more in the category of unquantifiable favors and concessions (or barter) than as transactions involving critical business assets having a quantifiable value.

In highly collaborative industries, customers and other business partners tie intellectual capital rights requests (often for know-how, design documentation, process documentation, and proprietary information of various kinds) to the purchase of goods and services from their suppliers, coercing the relinquishment of commercially unusual rights by dangling the promise of a purchase agreement for products and services. Without understanding the value of such intellectual capital rights, business-people—driven by orders and sales targets for products and services—will tend to provide commercially unusual intellectual capital rights as "sweeteners" to obtain product and service orders. And sometimes offering such "sweeteners" may be required for a company's short-term financial health or even its short-term survival.

In the supply chain context, customers, suppliers, co-development, and government agency partners are sources of angst because of their intellectual capital rights requests or demands. Often a company will pay a supplier to develop a product or to modify a product it already has. The supplier will often expect to retain all rights in such cases, arguing that the pre-existing intellectual capital and intellectual capital rights value is significantly greater than the value added by the customer's incremental investment. Sorting out the relative equities in such cases can require some real, fact-based analysis.

Sometimes, in order for a customer ultimately to pay a supplier for its products after a lengthy collaborative development period, that customer will sometimes require that the supplier cede ownership rights to the supplier's own product requirements and some of its product specification documentation. And this happens even when the customer has paid the supplier nothing for developing the requirements and specifications documents, nor for development of the product itself.

Again, particularly in the case of collaborative development efforts in collaborative industries, sorting out the relative value of the equities of the parties can be difficult. But it is necessary, if all parties to a collaborative development are to be treated fairly and if they are to receive a reasonable return on their investments. The alternative is naked market-power-based negotiations on intellectual capital rights.

Often, the business development manager or program manager assigned to lead a bid or the formation of a strategic alliance or a joint venture or some other business relationship will have little experience with or understanding of intellectual capital and its value. Such a person will often have little education concerning intellectual capital transactions. In these cases, an intellectual capital transaction expert can be a big help, facilitating appropriate strategic discussions, posing key questions, performing or supporting the intellectual capital valuations to do "what-if" analyses, helping to identify work-streams that may need to be accomplished to develop an intellectual capital strategy, setting up the meetings, keeping the action item log, and developing the action plan for tracking all the intellectual capital related questions and issues to ground.

For people unfamiliar with intellectual capital rights transactions, the basics concerning financial structures, normative kinds of rights to be considered, and effective deal structures will not be apparent. A cadre of intellectual capital transaction specialists can help here as well.

And sometimes in such transactions, the price of the intellectual capital rights in question—if any—sets the delegation of authority (the level in the organization that decides on pricing). So if the price of the intellectual capital rights is set at zero dollars, no one has to review the pricing. In theory, then, a low level program manager can choose to license or assign $100M in intellectual capital rights value (for example) without anyone knowing that he is doing so.

This can be a very big hole in the business policies and processes of a company. The delegation of authority for pricing intellectual capital rights should be determined by the value of the rights, when licensing out (or assignment out or assignment of joint ownership rights); and it should be set by the price of the rights when licensing in (or buying intellectual capital ownership rights). The organization responsible for the corporate policy regarding delegation of authority when considering intellectual capital rights should be our cadre of experts in intellectual capital management. And the procedure by which such rights are transacted should be owned by that same cadre of experts.

Additional Collaboration/Supply Chain Risk

As I say, in highly collaborative industries, intellectual capital rights bundles are often shared with one's co-development partners. Typically, these bundles evolve over the course of the development work. In other words, new intellectual capital is created, new discoveries are made, new test data is created, market conditions may change, and, potentially, the objectives of the parties may change. Even if the relationships are well-thought-out and are documented in sufficient detail in the implementing agreements, much new, unanticipated matter may be discovered and created in the course of any joint development work.

There are, therefore, two immediate areas for attention of the business and technical people involved with intellectual capital management in this circumstance. First, in the heat of development, most people on joint or co-development teams often forget what was originally agreed to regarding the divvying up of the intellectual capital rights and the documentation of that intellectual capital and the conveyance of it to the appropriate party or parties.

Alternatively, people on collaborative development teams won't have been thoroughly briefed in the first place on these matters and won't have been coached on how to manage the intellectual capital in this circumstance. In other words, there will be no (or little) business process agreed to by the parties to ensure that this new intellectual capital is properly documented and conveyed, as the collaborative development team progresses in its work. Without such business processes in place that are closely monitored, there frequently arise disagreements between and among the parties as to the real meaning of the terms regarding these issues in the governing agreements. A party or parties to such agreements may realize only after a period of many months or a few years that while their agreement gives them certain rights to the intellectual capital developed by another party, this promise is empty without the other party in fact adequately and sufficiently documenting the intellectual capital in question and adequately and sufficiently conveying it.

Such lags in the performance of the technology transfer provisions of the contractual agreement can result in quite destructive arguments and even legal action. So design of business processes that are tightly coupled with the contractual agreement, along with provisions and tools that ensure that throughout the technology or product development process the parties "true-up" their technology documentation and conveyance obligations, can be critical.

Second, in some collaborative developments, markets change, the technology in question changes, and the objectives of the parties may change. Again, developing effective business processes that are tightly coupled to the original contractual agreement and that allow for appropriate modifications to that agreement can be critical to avoiding deleterious conflict concerning the rights and obligations of the parties regarding the developing intellectual capital bundles.

Who has responsibility for developing, teaching, and monitoring such business processes in collaborative work? Too often, no one.

And as markets, technology, and objectives change, who has responsibility for valuing the intellectual capital rights bundle changes per the original agreement? Often, no one.

The role of business process design and changed intellectual capital rights valuation throughout the collaborative development process can certainly be provided by a representative of the cadre of intellectual capital management experts. In fact, it is likely that a standard set of business processes could be developed by such a group for application to the company's collaborative developments.

Pricing of Product- and Service-Based License Rights

In the business model section above, I mentioned a couple examples of various licensing-based business models (a number of which may be expressed as service agreements or subscription agreements). Of course, pricing for these licensing rights is difficult, since the variable cost of providing the incremental license rights is usually very small. In other words, one can't simply rely on the traditional hardware-based pricing model: beginning, for example, with the per unit or per subscriber variable cost, adding general and administrative expenses as a percentage of the unit variable cost, adding R&D as a percentage of the unit variable cost, and then tacking on other standard adders as a percentage of the unit variable cost, along with an appropriate percentage-based profit before tax.

When people are attempting to develop pricing for these sorts of licensing businesses, it can be helpful to find similar-to licensing scenarios and similar-to functionality in the market upon which to base a competitive price. These are called "comparables" and are the foundation of market-based value analysis. But if one is first to market with a unique and differentiated licensed product or service, one has a conundrum, if one is not knowledgeable about intellectual capital valuation techniques and approaches and if one is not cognizant of the literature in the field. Without such a background, one may be reduced to playing a pure guessing game, which can be exciting but perhaps not as fulfilling (in a financial sense) as one might like.

I remember working with a product line guy a number of years ago to develop an assessment of the intellectual capital value in a software product that the engineering team was getting ready to release to the market. Customers had been asking for pricing. The product had been under development for a couple of years, and of course, I had a matter of a few weeks to produce an assessment. We had a number of meetings, in which I asked for a variety of kinds of data relating to the product's potential economic value from the customer's perspective and was told that the data I wanted wasn't available and wasn't attainable within the required time. I suggested a survey or a focus group with industry decision makers and influencers. But this would take 2-3 months to put together and would cost between $50,000 and $70,000 to execute.

(In the case of this particular software product, the $100,000 investment in development would have been recouped within a month or two and could have potentially added many hundreds of thousands of dollars to the business unit's bottom line over a period of a couple of years.)

We had looked around for comparables, but no one was in the market with something close to what we had. I wanted to do an economic benefit assessment, but as I say, the data wasn't available for that.

Frustrated, the product line guy got with the marketing guy and they came up with a number for me. What they did was to take all kinds of software products that did something in the same general field of what their product did, falling way short in many cases, or doing functions that were so different as to evoke a lot of head-scratching on my part. I think there were about eight or nine of them. What the two of them did was to total all of their prices up and take an average. (And of course, the original pricing on many of these products had been done with all the rigor of a series of coin flips.)

It was as if to find a market price of a room in a well-outfitted ice hotel in Barrow, Alaska, we had determined the rental rates of the following and then taken the average:

- A room in an unimproved home built in the 1930s in Nutley, New Jersey
- A brand new 3,000 square foot house in Laguna Beach, California
- The Museum of Modern Art in New York City
- An ice fishing hut on Lake Winnibigoshish, in Minnesota
- The presidential suite at the Ritz Carlton in Dubai
- A tiny house (200 square feet) on a trailer, parked in Topinabee, Michigan
- A houseboat on Lake Meade
- A vintage Airstream trailer parked in Gulf Shores, Alabama
- A room in the sleeping car on the California Zephyr

Ultimately, a comparables analysis can be done effectively or ineffectively, and this is an example of how to do an ineffective comparables analysis. In fact, this way of doing things is completely irrelevant to the question of value that we are trying to answer. If this approach is used, we will find ourselves going over Niagara Falls without a paddle...or a parachute...or a barrel.

Business-Process-Based License Rights

Often a business partner or the U.S. government or a foreign government (or one of their surrogate companies) may want to license a company's business processes. Perhaps these are engineering processes, manufacturing processes, supplier management processes, quality management processes, investment decision-making processes, testing and qualification processes, and/or risk mitigation processes, among others. My experience with business and technical people's qualitative assessment of the value of such processes is that they are not worth anything much. The common business and technical view is that these kinds of processes are shared broadly across many different companies and industries and that one company's particular way of doing business doesn't much differ from another company's way of doing business.

There are text-books and management framework standards that are widely published on this sort of intellectual capital. Remarkably—as I say—most business-people think that there isn't much value in it.

It's one thing to read about the requirements for these sorts of business processes and the tools for implementing them in text books and standards documents, but it's quite another to put together an optimal set of business processes tailored for the actual operation of a particular enterprise to meet these requirements. Actual implemented and effective processes are typically developed over years or decades. Their starting point may be in published standards documents or business texts, but to create and maintain a company that operates smoothly and efficiently takes a great deal of effort, involving many disciplines, many organizations, and many people reaching across organizational boundaries. (Reaching across organizational boundaries can, of course, itself be hard.)

In highly regulated industries, these business processes are quite involved and may take many years to develop. And in such industries, business processes go hand-in-hand with reputation (brand), which again is built incrementally with government agencies, regulatory authorities, and enterprise business partners over a period of years or decades. The investment required in building an interlocking network of enterprise business processes to meet regulatory and statutory demands can be formidable, running to hundreds of millions or billions of dollars.

In fact, the cost of developing, maintaining, and improving such business processes can sometimes overshadow product technology investments. The value of business-process-based intellectual capital rights can dwarf the value of the rights to specific products or services. (Examples may be FedEx, Amazon, and Google.)

What business processes did Apple develop back in the 1990s that resulted in hit after hit, successful innovation after innovation? What business processes did Microsoft develop from the 1990s through the decade of the 20-teens that enabled it to reinvent itself and remain relevant? What about Walmart? What about Amazon?

How do such companies thrive in a very fast-moving, bet-your-company market? Great CEOs? Well, great CEOs can work for lousy companies and deliver lousy results. When a company operates on the scale of these, its business processes have to be wide, deep, and working well. Its business processes have to keep the company innovative and nimble, despite the company's size. They have to be robust to weather the comings and goings of various business leaders, with their peculiarities, weaknesses, and whimseys. And the human capital—the know-how of key contributors—will have to be excellent.

Can you imagine one of these latter highly innovative technology-based companies licensing its key business process intellectual capital to a joint venture in China? Not likely. But industrial companies are doing so and have been doing so regularly for decades. A cadre of business-people who are expert in intellectual capital rights valuation, quantitative risk assessments, and the creation of intellectual capital management business processes can be helpful in understanding and managing the implications of this sort of intellectual capital licensing.

Cybersecurity, Physical Security, and Compartmentalization

Of course, there are experts in cybersecurity and physical security, and they play an outsized role in the development and application of technical approaches by which intellectual capital is protected through non-legal means. In recognition of the hacker threat and insider threat to companies' intellectual capital, most boards of directors have created committees to address these threats. These risks are regarded as important and are taken seriously in most publicly traded companies.

But one of the issues with asking technologists to lead what is essentially a business process design is that they will tend to be heavy on the technology and light on the business processes and on change management and communication around those new business processes. This may also be an area where a cadre of intellectual capital management experts can help.

Inevitably there will be many stakeholders across the enterprise and many organizations that will be touched by business processes designed to stop internal and external threats to a company's intellectual capital. Tradeoffs will need to be made. Costs and inconvenience will need to be balanced with levels of effectiveness. Intellectual capital will need to be differentially managed, depending on its value to the enterprise—more care given and more expensive approaches taken to protecting the more valuable intellectual capital. This of course means that someone—or more likely, a diverse group of knowledgeable people—will need to assess the relative value of the intellectual capital to be protected.

Teams of users, technologists, and business-people—people skilled in efficient, effective business process design and deployment—need to participate. Change management and communication experts need to help straighten the way for changes in business processes to be accepted and implemented quickly and effectively. And because the threats are always changing, the technology is always improving, and business users are always learning how to do things better, such processes will need to be updated regularly.

Have I mentioned compartmentalization? Compartmentalization is one of the most generally effective non-legal (business process) methods of limiting the effect of an attempt to compromise a company's intellectual capital. In business processes designed to limit the risk of intellectual capital theft and misuse, compartmentalization is always at the heart of the work.

None of this happens magically. Business processes require real effort and care to design well and to maintain. Most people in most organizations don't want to be inconvenienced. As a result, designing, implementing, and maintaining business processes to protect a company's intellectual capital can be counter-cultural. And in such cases the most difficult aspect of the work is in changing the culture.

Valuation Specialty Centers

If there are intellectual capital licensing scenarios that are repeated frequently, with little variation in key parameters, perhaps it would make sense for the intellectual capital management team to establish valuation specialty centers. This would entail training a team who would value the regularly licensed type of intellectual capital. By doing so, the intellectual capital experts would be able to delegate valuation responsibilities to others to free themselves up to do other, more complex intellectual capital valuation work. Candidate organizations in which to place this capability would be the business unit finance function or a product area management group within the business management function. It's probably best for the senior finance and business management leaders to work out where (organizationally) they would prefer for this function to reside.

Strategic Investment

As I've mentioned previously, understanding intellectual capital rights value can help in assessing various investment opportunities, comparing and contrasting one against the other. A cadre of intellectual capital valuation experts, working with technology, product, strategy, and market experts, can help analyze various strategically important investment options. The objective here is to assess the best place to put the company's investment dollars. To make this assessment, one wants to know what the likely payoff would be to making certain sorts of technology bets. People who are used to assessing technology (intellectual capital) value in various scenarios with differing discount rate profiles and other key assumptions can be helpful.

Bid-Based Rights Alternatives

Often, in a business-to-business bid situation, a company is asked by a customer to give up commercially unusual rights to its intellectual capital, in order for the bidder to win an opportunity to sell products and services to that customer. To conduct a reasoned and reasonable discussion and negotiation, the bidder should understand the differential value of the various rights alternatives that should be considered. Assessing those various values can become an important part of the internal consensus-building process for formulating an intellectual capital rights offer. Doing so can also become an important part of the process by which the bidder conducts its discussions and negotiations with the customer. So, a cadre of experts in intellectual capital rights valuation and deal structure alternatives can be of help here to the generalist business-people leading the bid and decision-making processes.

Public Policy

Every industry has at least one or perhaps several trade associations that monitor industry legislation and regulation at the national level. The company's representation on the intellectual capital committees and councils of such organizations can be important, and the company's support of the education of Congressional staffers, Congressional members, and regulatory personnel can make a significant difference in the laws and regulations that ultimately impinge upon the company's operating success and business models. This is an ongoing need, with countervailing forces often trying to undo, and sometimes succeeding in undoing, the beneficial legislative and regulatory achievements that such company intellectual capital strategy specialists have made.

I think of this work as similar to the work of Sisyphus, who was doomed by the gods—according to Greek mythology and more recently Albert Camus—to roll a very heavy rock up a mountain, only to have the rock roll down to the bottom of the mountain, once it had reached the top. Of course, Sisyphus must—because he was doomed by the gods to do so—roll the great rock up the mountain once again. And again. And again. Infinitely. This work is therefore character-building in a hellacious sort of way. It requires the combined talents of the business strategists, lobbyists, intellectual capital experts, and lawyers; so, any cadre of company intellectual capital experts should expect to support and perhaps to lead such work for the company.

Standards

In some companies, the intellectual capital management experts lead the technical standards work, since it is both strategic (advantaging the company's technology in the marketplace of products and services) and also potentially income-generating through the licensing of standards-essential patents (SEPs) to one's competitors. Most companies regard technical standards as the purview of the engineering department, but that department may not have responsibility for the company's product-market strategy and may or may not be tightly coupled into developing and implementing that product-market strategy.

When technical standards and product-market strategy become de-coupled, unfortunate things can happen. And when the technical standards strategy is not closely coupled with the intellectual capital strategy for an important product line or service—or with the revenue and profit generation strategy for licensing SEPs—bad things may happen as well. This suggests the importance of involving the intellectual capital management experts in this important work as well.

As I mention in a few pages, there is additionally the realm of intellectual capital management standards work. The intellectual capital management experts should certainly be involved with strategies pertaining to such standards, as well as the development of them, their enterprise implementation, and any conformance certification work.

Knowledge Management

Some companies have in place formal or informal ways of managing knowledge. Technology areas, business process areas, product areas and others can be the focus of these activities. Some companies structure on-line communities within the companies' intranet. Others support a combination of in-person and virtual communities. In both cases, there may be regular meetings, formal presentations on various topics, panel discussions, lessons learned sessions, internal publications of various kinds, and so forth. These activities are designed to enhance the knowledge of others who have the same or similar interests or responsibilities and can have the effect of improving the professional knowledge and skill of people with related interests across the enterprise. In such companies, a cadre of intellectual capital management experts could structure knowledge dissemination sessions targeted at various constituencies throughout the company, focused on the management of intellectual capital.

Communication

A cadre of intellectual capital management experts should also consider setting up regular communications originating from its own members on various topics designed to raise the awareness of the value of intellectual capital, potential risks to the company's intellectual capital, methods of extracting value from the company's intangible assets, reasonable and unreasonable approaches to the negotiation of intellectual capital rights, reasonable and unreasonable ways to approach the valuation of intellectual capital rights, and so forth. This ought to be done in an entertaining way, with a light touch. The idea here is to get key employees to open and actually read or watch the communication and to look forward to it, in part because of its entertainment value.

I'm echoing the project undertaken by Joseph Addison and Richard Steele in their creation of *The Spectator*, which was published from 1711 until 1712. The objective of this work was "to enliven morality with wit and to temper wit with morality." Of course, the way we might think about an intra-company communication project on the topic of intellectual capital management today will have a bit more focus on changing the hearts and minds of company employees concerning the way they are managing the company's intellectual capital and to establish (or re-establish) norms around the expected practices.

But again, we will want a light touch here—we want humor and even some silliness (not something companies are typically good at or good at allowing) and enough novelty to be inherently interesting—to motivate people to open and receive the communication. References to popular culture—movies, TV shows, books, etc.—may be helpful in providing both levity and common anchor points for people to grasp a field that is so invisible and indistinct and vague.

The Future

What all the above amounts to is a series of possible steps in the direction of a more comprehensive business and financial management system for intellectual capital, with a specific focus on structural capital: particularly proprietary information, technology, business processes of all sorts, product design documentation, customized enterprise resource management systems, enterprise software tools and frameworks, and intangible-based products and services (based on proprietary software and information, for example). Are there other steps one might take? Certainly, but I'm focused here on areas that may benefit from a contribution of enhanced expertise in companies I'm familiar with—the low hanging fruit of the Preface. Of course, that's not to say these concepts can't be applied across virtually any company and arguably in all industries.

As I say, my emphasis is on certain aspects of intellectual capital management. I haven't prioritized human capital management and relationship capital management in the discussion above because these areas have been and continue to be resourced fairly well by knowledgeable people in the organizations with which I'm familiar. I suppose the one caveat is that relationship capital and human capital could be managed much more effectively with input from an intellectual capital management cadre in the context of transactions with customers, suppliers, co-development partners, and government agencies when intellectual capital rights are a key component of these relationships.

With all that having been said, I'm imagining enterprises in the future with the following overlapping effective expertise and business processes in the area of structural capital management:

- Financial analysis of intangibles-based (e.g., software and information) products and services business models
- Valuation of both technology-based and intangible-products-and-services-based intellectual capital rights in transactions
- Limitation of enterprise intellectual capital releases to other entities only when and to the extent necessary and limitation of the receipt of intellectual capital from others only when and to the extent necessary
- Education and mentoring provided to those business-people expected to develop and negotiate intellectual capital rights agreements with others
- Effective compartmentalization and control of intellectual capital inside the enterprise and inside the enterprise's business partners that have access to enterprise intellectual capital
- Metrics that measure the enterprise's innovativeness and efficiency in converting its innovations into sales and profits, at a low enough level (at the level of specific products and services) that it is meaningful to the management of the business
- Provision of business partner requirements in the custodianship of enterprise intellectual capital that are at least as rigorously developed and applied as any other business partner requirements

- Implementation of relevant intellectual capital management standards developed by credible intellectual capital management standards developers: i.e., either ISO or LES
- An intellectual capital management audit program applied both internally and externally that is appropriately rigorous and frequent
- Development and application of intellectual capital strategy in an integrated way with the development and application of the company's business strategy

The Present

But what about the present? Where are we today regarding a disciplined approach to the management of intellectual capital in our companies, our business partners, and our transactions? Perhaps if we look at the way we are organized and the way our work is focused today in a couple of other areas and remove that focus as an experiment—a thought experiment—we might get some perspective on the reason developing a cadre of intellectual capital management experts would make sense. We consider such a thought experiment in the next chapter.

Chapter Five:
A Thought Experiment

To me, wearing glasses is no pleasure, but once I conceded that I simply couldn't properly judge distance without them, I began to experiment. I tried glasses and found them uncomfortable. I switched to contact lenses, and they also bothered me.

—**Arnold Palmer:** *GOLF* Magazine

I don't think that you can invent on behalf of customers unless you're willing to think long-term, because a lot of invention doesn't work. If you're going to invent, it means you're going to experiment, and if you're going to experiment, you're going to fail, and if you're going to fail, you have to think long term.

—**Jeff Bezos:** *GeekWire*

A Very Short Story: Henry Ford was born on his family's farm on July 30, 1863, in Greenfield Township, Michigan. In his teens, he was known as an excellent pocket watch repairman. In 1879, he left for Detroit to become an apprentice machinist. He moved around from job to job, learning as he went and building prototype vehicles in his spare time. Through this prototyping experience, he learned how not to make automobiles. Eventually, he founded the Ford Motor Company and built and sold several models—the A, B, C, F, K, and N—as his engineering and manufacturing teams experimented with various design and manufacturing processes—ways to define, organize, and divide up the work within an enterprise. At first a team of about 15 men built the vehicle in place. Then one man built the entire vehicle from its component parts, with others bringing the parts to him. Next, the Ford team arrayed many build stations in a line and had specialists move from build station to build station affixing a particular component or subsystem to the developing vehicles. There were other perturbations, with a variety of accompanying inventory management and delivery schemes. Then as Ford and his team designed and prepared to build the model T, they sought a manufacturing model that would have the continuous flow characteristic of the Chicago slaughter-houses, where cows and pigs were killed and disassembled progressively as they were moved by overhead trolleys past workers who were specialized in removing various parts of the animals. This was the Ford team's great insight. Using the principal of reverse analogy, they asked themselves: Why not assemble vehicles using a similar process, moving the vehicle components and subsystems past workers who specialized in assembling them and then attaching them to the vehicle? This approach was first implemented at the Model T factory in Highland Park, Michigan (where my grandfather worked for many years, back in the day of the Model T and afterwards, into the 1950s). The efficiency that was achieved over the nearly 20 years of the model T's manufacture was evident in its price. Initially, it was priced at about $850, and at the end of its production life, it was priced at about $260.

The moral of the story? Perhaps it is this: some of the biggest breakthroughs in business management theory and practice have come through analogy, even reverse analogy.

In many enterprises today, there seems to be an expectation that the lawyers are managing the intellectual capital. But that is usually not the case. They do have an obligation to manage business processes related to securing intellectual property law protection and contractual law protection and enforcing those legal protections. But they are usually not expected, for example, to put into place business processes by which research and development investments and invention and commercialization processes result in optimal financial outcomes for a company. Perhaps some lawyers would like this responsibility and authority, but in most cases, this does not happen.

Lawyers are not expected to develop business models that might optimally capture value from the company's intellectual capital. They are not expected to assess the value of intellectual capital rights or to work with the compliance team to ensure that accurate and justifiable purchase price allocation is performed when mergers and acquisitions activities come along. They are not expected to coordinate the cross-enterprise activities of the information technology team, the physical security team, the engineering and business development and program management and strategy folks, and the contracts and subcontracts organizations to develop coherent business processes for managing sensitive intellectual capital belonging to business partners as well as the company itself. (While the lawyers typically have responsibility for helping to develop and implement the business processes of the contracts and subcontracts organizations, they typically do not have cross-enterprise business process development and implementation responsibilities involving all the other disciplines as well.)

These cross-enterprise sorts of activities are the purview of the business management people: business strategists, profit and loss center managers, program managers, product line managers, business developers, marketing people, engineering managers, financial managers, procurement people, and so forth.

But often these people—who are actually doing (or not doing) a company's intellectual capital management—are not schooled in the management of intellectual capital. Sometimes they do not understand what the predictability and reliability of the relevant intellectual property law and contractual law would be in multiple jurisdictions. (And in a global company this is critical business (profit-and-loss center) knowledge.) Many do not understand how to apply financial analytical frameworks to intellectual-capital-based business models.

Many have difficulty identifying the forms or examples of intellectual capital. Some have little insight into the ability of others to gain access to a company's intellectual capital and to make profitable use of it. Many are not schooled in what reasonable expectations might be concerning prudent custodianship of a company's intellectual capital and the prudent custodianship of business partners' intellectual capital.

Only some are experienced in developing and managing relationships with business partners in which the question of intellectual capital rights is a major element of the relationship. And only some have insight into the financial value of intellectual capital rights.

My thesis, then, is that intellectual capital can be managed much better than it currently is in some (perhaps many) companies. With better knowledge and insight, better skills, better analytical approaches, better business processes, better organizational design, and clearer organizational accountability and responsibility, companies could improve their long-term financial performance through better intellectual capital management.

Do I have direct evidence of this? I have a lot of specific personal knowledge and experience with this that is proprietary to the companies for which I have toiled. There is some publicly available evidence. For example, there is evidence from the world of patent licensing (licensing of the legal rights to one form of technology). Some companies have significantly improved their financial performance through a focus on patent licensing, particularly those who license patents that read on technical standards. Certainly, there are a number of companies that have done business in China and have had their intellectual capital rights misappropriated to the significant detriment of their businesses. So we have some positive and some negative evidence.

But beyond the headlines and court cases, perhaps one can get a sense of the scope of the possible benefit of doing intellectual capital management better by taking a look at a couple of other discipline areas within the 21st century company.

What non-obvious subsets of structural (business processes) and human capital (know-how) provide substantial input to the equity value of a company, similar to the more obvious forms of structural and human capital contributions that we have discussed? What about the management systems concerning the performance of the company's employees? And what about the way the company manages the flow of money through itself? (We are going to get a little recursive here, but that's okay. Please stay with me.)

Let's take people first. What would happen if we didn't have a human resources management department? What if all human resources (HR) management matters were left up to individual managers? What if recruiting, compliance training, enterprise education, specialized knowledge training, leadership training, compensation structures, position level structures, special monetary awards, long term incentive compensation, bonuses, performance assessments, disciplinary policies, termination policies, sexual harassment policies and training, employee intellectual capital ownership and license rights, employee contractual obligations, and so forth were all up to individual managers and departments? What if there were few or no enterprise-wide policies, processes, and tools for the management of employees? What if there were no human resources cadre?

What if all or almost all HR matters were left up to individual managers and departments and there were merely a small group of lawyers who lurched from compliance issue to compliance issue and from labor law issue to labor law issue providing legal guidance? Wouldn't this be similar to how intellectual capital is managed today in many companies?

The premise of such an *ad hoc*, distributed approach seems to be that—in most of structural capital management—no specialists are needed (outside of the intellectual property lawyers), that no central authority is needed, that no or very few enterprise-wide business policies, processes, or tools are required, that there are no (and should not be any) business experts in the various aspects of structural capital management, and that no enterprise-wide metrics would be useful or beneficial.

And now, let's consider the management of the flow of money through the organization and between the company and other enterprises. Again, let's perform a thought experiment and assume a company without a centralized finance and accounting organization. Let's assume that there is no cadre of specialists assigned to managing the flow of money, outside of the attorneys managing the company's interaction with the US government's attorneys at the Securities and Exchange Commission, Department of Justice, and Federal Trade Commission.

In such an organization, there would be no enterprise-wide approach to revenue recognition, to the management of debits and credits, to financial decision-making authority. In such an organization, all departments would be on their own to figure out how to satisfy the SEC/FASB accounting rules, and the people hired to do this work would be generalists—people without backgrounds in accounting standards. In this case, formulating quarterly and annual financial results for the company would be an exercise in *ad hoc* invention and extemporaneous guestimates.

The reporting process would be full of anxiety and emotion. There would be conflicts among portions of the enterprise as to who owes what information to whom, when. There would be inconsistencies and significant miscommunication. Since accounting concepts and language would not be commonly understood across parts of the organization—because the people handling accounting tasks would not be educated in accounting—the organization would have no way of conducting its financial business in an orderly way. People would routinely talk past each other. There would be no common accounting vocabulary.

Sound familiar? This is what structural capital management looks like in many companies: *ad hoc* and catch-as-catch-can.

But let us briefly entertain a third thought experiment. What if the legal department were put in charge of human resources or put in charge of finance and accounting? Isn't this like putting the legal department in charge of structural capital management? Wouldn't they bring similar knowledge and understanding to the task? Wouldn't enterprises likely obtain similar results? Lawyers can be excellent at managing the legal aspects of things, but how much education have they had in human resources management? How about finance and accounting? Not much, right?

How much education have they had and how much reading have they done in the field of intellectual capital management—in the management of our investments in our human capital, relationship capital, and structural capital and in the extraction of value from those investments? In other words, how much education and experience have they had with managing business and financial matters? How much experience have they had with managing a profit-and-loss center, generating orders, sales, and profits for the company, making investment decisions, and modeling the financials of all of this? Not much, I expect.

Are any of these constructs reasonable? Does the way many companies handle the management of intellectual capital pass the reasonableness test? If the value of the asset class were minimal, I'd say yes. But it turns out that the value of this asset class is somewhere between 60 and 90 percent of most companies' equity value.

So *ad hoc* and catch-as-catch-can won't work. Putting the business management of intellectual capital in the hands of the legal department doesn't seem appropriate. Not for much longer. There are too many savvy lawyers out there, itching to launch shareholder suits. There is too much competition. There are too many competitors willing to radically reformulate business models and governance and innovation management structures and practices. There are too many companies and government entities with greatly asymmetric market power who are willing to prey upon their business partners and strip their differentiating intellectual capital rights from them in return for promises of diminishing or nonexistent new product sales and profits.

The question now becomes, what direct evidence do we have that the current approach to intellectual capital management is suboptimal? Are there data we can look at? Do we have only analogy—or reverse analogy—to rely upon? Our next chapter addresses these questions.

Chapter Six:
Regular Disorder

Turning and turning in the widening gyre
The falcon cannot hear the falconer;
Things fall apart; the centre cannot hold;
Mere anarchy is loosed upon the world,
The blood-dimmed tide is loosed, and everywhere
The ceremony of innocence is drowned;
The best lack all conviction, while the worst
Are full of passionate intensity.

—**W.B. Yeats:** "The Second Coming"

A Very Short Story: The Laurel and Hardy film, *The Music Box*, won the first Academy Award for Best Live Action Short (Comedy) in 1932. In it, Laurel and Hardy have gone into business with $3.80 of savings to "re-organize and re-supervise their entire financial structure," and have founded the Laurel and Hardy Transfer Company. This company appears to have tangible assets of one horse and a freight wagon and some sort of relationship capital with at least one music instrument store, along with the human capital of Stan Laurel and Oliver Hardy themselves— their particular professional knowledge and skill. (One might argue in this particular case that the value of the human capital may be a negative number, but I will leave that out of the present story.) The company is engaged to deliver an upright piano to 1127 Walnut Street. The piano is a surprise birthday gift from a woman to her husband. Upon nearing their destination with the piano, our indeterminate duo asks the postman about the location of the address, and he points them up a staircase leading about 70 feet up a hill to the home in question. What he doesn't tell them is that a street climbs the hill and presents the visitor or delivery person at the front door of the abode, which is around the other side and not visible from the bottom of the hill. Laurel and Hardy proceed to push, carry, and drop the piano multiple times up and down the long staircase, expostulating all the way. And then the recipient, once the piano is delivered—who hates pianos—dismantles what remains of the gift with an axe.

The moral of this story? Perhaps it is this: one might benefit from a critical, multi-perspective look at the question of business management. The first or current or most obvious path may not be the optimal path.

Managing—or attempting to manage—intellectual capital in the 21st century enterprise is difficult. Some might say it is a fool's errand. This may be hyperbole.

Managing intellectual capital is an emotional business, characterized by a lack of orderliness. Many people charged with the management of a company's intellectual capital have little idea that they are in fact charged with the management of the company's intellectual capital. They do not know what intellectual capital is. They do not have a vocabulary and tools with which to understand and to manage many aspects of a company's intellectual capital store.

I say it's an emotional business because when people don't have a good grasp on what they are doing—and they're supposed to—they become defensive. Emotion becomes a way to respond to one's own recognition that one is ignorant of something important. And one's lack of knowledge in this particular area has real consequences.

As I've mentioned, the mean percentage of companies' equity value ascribable to intellectual capital is variously pegged at between 60 and 90 percent. (There are many references that one might cite for this claim, one of which is the following publication available as a PDF on-line: *What Ideas Are Worth: The Value of Intellectual Capital and Intangible Assets in the American Economy*, by Kevin A. Hassett and Robert J. Shapiro.)

Yet intellectual capital management—structural capital management, specifically—is not taught in most business schools. When it is taught as a management discipline (in the rare instance), it is usually taught by adjuncts of various sorts, not tenured professors. It is taught by practitioners rather than by people doing or supervising research. In other words, there is no broadly recognized sub-discipline of structural capital management within the broader discipline of business management in most business schools.

No wonder some business and financial leaders in enterprises today don't know what structural capital is or how to manage it systematically. No wonder structural capital management is sometimes an emotional business.

(I do want to acknowledge that not all business leaders and all companies have this fundamental hole in their understanding. There are some exceptional products and services companies who are very good at generating and managing innovation and integrating their structural capital strategy with their business strategy. And of course, businesses that historically have had intellectual capital licensing at the heart of their business model may often be excellent in the management of their structural capital.)

In addition, there have been no generally accepted business management standards established in the field. I think of quality management, risk management, human resources management, and financial reporting management as subset areas, and of course these fields are taught. You can find courses on this stuff. And there are management framework standards relating to each of them. Not so with most of the rest of intellectual capital management.

I say the lack of knowledge about structural capital management has real consequences, and what I mean is, for example, that somewhere between $225B and $600B in structural capital value is stolen or misappropriated from U.S. companies every year. (This is the finding of the 2017 *Update to the IP Commission Report—The Theft of American Intellectual Property: Reassessments of the Challenge and United States Policy.* This *IP Commission Report* was co-chaired by Dennis C. Blair and Jon M. Huntsman, Jr. Their report may also be found on-line as a PDF.)

Further, if most of the people who are charged with managing their company's structural capital don't know what structural capital is, you can bet that, in addition to letting it flow like water through a sieve and into the hands of their competitors, they may not be optimizing its value in the marketplace. Yes, there are tools available to help business management people assess the productivity of their investments. A useful calculation in this regard is return on investment (ROI). But how often is this actually used on a project-by-project or technology-bundle-by-technology-bundle basis? And how often is it actually applied in a systematic, risk-adjusted way in the management of a business?

This is difficult to know, but anecdotally we hear that much of U.S. research and development is not exposed at the project level to financial analysis.

In addition, when intellectual capital rights are licensed or sold, there is also no regular order, except the order (if you would like to call it that) that Congress, the courts, and agencies of the executive branch impose on the economic actors in the economy. For example, even for well-defined categories of intellectual capital—such as inventions protected by patents—many in these institutions and agencies do not know what they are doing, either. They think about the issues only periodically and at a very high level. Being generalists, many have not studied this stuff. Many have not read the books, written the articles, spoken at the conferences, taught the courses, and written the books that constitute the underpinnings of the field. Neither, in general, have the staffs that support them.

(There are exceptions here. One of the more remarkable positive exceptions is the US Patent and Trademark Office (PTO). I have found the people in the PTO to be generally very knowledgeable and exceptionally diligent. And there are certainly experts in intellectual capital matters working in a wide variety of other federal agencies, but I haven't seen their expertise consistently drive policy. In other words, policy matters seem to be managed mostly by people who are interested in prioritizing other perceived goods. As to Congress and Congressional staff, their legislative priorities seem to be elsewhere as well.)

Asking Congress, the courts, and agencies of the Executive Branch to impose regular and beneficent order on the intellectual capital marketplace is like asking them to design a computer's operating system or to organize a company's supply chain or develop an enterprise's business model. They can do these things, if pressured, but not necessarily very well. For the most part, most also have no meaningful education or experience in the management of intellectual capital.

I recall hearing a federal district court judge—one of the first in the country to preside in a case on the licensing of standard essential patents (patents that are required to practice a particular technical standard)—saying that he and the jury in the case had no idea of how to value the patents. (In the case in question, one company had sued another for infringing its standard essential patents, and the plaintiff and defendant had disagreed about whether there were economic damages and, if so, how they should be calculated.) The judge pointed out that judges and juries are educated in much different matters. So why didn't the experts weigh in pre-emptively and sort these issues out for the generalists? Why is the value of patent rights a question for judges and juries rather than a question for intellectual capital rights valuation experts and the affected companies? Don't they have a better handle on how to look at the problem from an economic perspective than a judge or jury or both?

Of course, he and judges similarly situated in infringement cases have a universe of experts in intellectual capital valuation to rely on. So what I think he may have been implying is that because each side in an intellectual capital rights case will present experts at trial that are biased toward their client's interests, they are likely to give the court biased assessments of value. I think he was saying that he is not sufficiently expert in the valuation of intellectual capital rights (often patent rights, but not always, by any means) to sort out whom or what to believe. Finally, what I think he was implying is that there ought to be common methodologies, common ways to arrive at common assumptions, and valuation results from different practitioners that should not differ by a country mile.

I'm reminded of a passage in a remarkable book by Ronald K. Fierstein—*A Triumph of Genius: Edwin Land, Polaroid, and the Kodak Patent War.* The Honorable A. David Mazzone presided over the damages portion of the *Polaroid v. Kodak* litigation. Fierstein, who was on the Polaroid litigation team, writes the following: "After hearing bewildering and conflicting opinions from many expert witnesses on both sides, Judge Mazzone clearly felt that the two parties should have reached a settlement and not relied on a court to resolve issues that were more economic and business-related than legal" (p. 503).

I also recall a panel discussion in a conference not too long ago in which a retired chief justice of the Court of Appeals for the Federal Circuit (the one dedicated federal appeals court for intellectual property matters) said that the experts should be designing the operation of the nation's intellectual capital management system, not the generalists in Congress, the courts, and the agencies of the executive branch, for the same reasons offered by the district court judge above.

Further, Baruch Lev, in his book, *The End of Accounting and the Path Forward for Investors and Managers* (2016), points out that the financial statements of publicly traded companies no longer reflect the realities of business and that they picture an alternative financial reality that fails to illuminate essential factors relevant to companies' future success or failure. Important evidence of his thesis is the accounting treatment of the cost of value-creating investments in intellectual capital generally.

Modern accounting systems treat investment in intellectual capital as they do the payment of rents or the purchase of office supplies. The value of most intellectual capital, which underpins 60 to 90 percent of the value of the twenty-first century corporation, is treated by our accounting practices today as extinguished, as soon as it is paid for.

This means that when internal investments that were made in the past are considered for use on a current or future project or transaction of some sort, the fruits of these investments—the resulting intellectual capital—are considered to be free to the project or to the team executing the transaction. In other words, the people employing intellectual capital rights that have already been paid for are free to use those rights often with no (or little) accountability—whether to company leadership or to the shareholders.

This of course makes no sense. It is as if the company purchased real estate for $100M but then said to a project team or a deal team that it would be fine if this real estate were to be given away for free. Up to the team.

No wonder business leaders have a difficult time understanding what intellectual capital is and how to manage it well. Accounting practices imply that it is worthless. Investment and management practices imply that it is worthless. So why bother with it? Why would anyone volunteer to be accountable for management of a worthless, non-existent asset?

There is no regular order in any of this. What we have is regular disorder, a disorder so profound that setting things to rights seems…well, a fool's errand.

But I remain hopeful. One of the reasons is—as I've mentioned above—powerful and helpful standards that have been developed to aid in the field of business management. They are an existence proof. If standards can be developed in those fields, why not in the management of the company's intellectual capital—its structural capital in particular. In the next chapter, we take up this possibility.

Chapter Seven:
Standards

Intellectual property has the shelf life of a banana.
      —**Bill Gates:** *The Wall Street Journal* (Dec. 29, 2011)

If you can't describe what you are doing as a process, you don't know what you are doing.
      —**W. Edwards Deming:** Source unknown

A Very Short Story: W. Edwards Deming was born on October 14, 1900, in Sioux City, Iowa. He was raised on farms in Polk County, Iowa, and Powell, Wyoming. His undergraduate degree was in electrical engineering, while his graduate degrees were in mathematics and physics. For a substantial portion of his career, he was a professor in New York University's graduate school of business and consulted with businesses globally on business management systems, with a particular emphasis on quality management. He has been recognized by the Japanese government and by Japanese businesses as a major contributor to Japan's industrial rebirth and its worldwide economic success in the 1950s and 1960s. In his book, *Out of Crisis* (1986), he wrote, "Long-term commitment to new learning and new philosophy is required of any management that seeks transformation. The timid and the fainthearted, and the people that expect quick results, are doomed to disappointment." He is widely regarded as one of the principal promulgators of quality management philosophy, and his work has been credited, in part, with the global success enjoyed by the ISO 9001 quality management standard.

The moral of this story? Perhaps there are several: business management innovation is open to anyone, even mathematicians and physicists. Human persistence—like rain on the tallest mountains—can be transformative, given sufficient time. What can seem a waste of time to some, may turn out to be a key competitive advantage to others.

One of the emerging areas of value contribution for intellectual capital management experts is standards. I say "emerging" because there haven't been many standards created in the field of intellectual capital management as of this writing. But there are quite a few in the works, and there needs to be somewhere in the enterprise where experts on these standards may reside and where decisions would be made about whether the enterprise should (1) employ such standards informally or (2) elect both to employ such standards and to be certified to be in conformance with such standards. And there needs to be a group in the enterprise that leads development and implementation of enterprise policies and processes (and documentation) to ensure the enterprise is in conformance with the selected standards.

To some, the concept of a standard or a family of standards for intellectual capital management seems nonsensical. People understand technical standards: they allow companies to cooperate on common design or performance elements and interfaces in hardware and software so that together these companies can create a coherent product market in which all may compete. But what could an intellectual capital management standard entail? What would it be used for? Why would it be useful?

In addition to technical standards, there is a rather large realm of endeavor in the standards world that is variously described as business process standards or management framework standards. Perhaps the most well-known of these is the ISO 9001 quality management standard. It is used across all business types and sizes and across the world to aid in the creation of enterprise-based quality management systems. You might think of the standard itself as a set of requirements for the design of business processes that are used to manage an enterprise's product quality. It is a vehicle for teaching enterprises about product quality and product quality management systems and is the mechanism by which people from across the globe share lessons learned and develop consensus on how to improve product quality systems—which are, in fact, business processes.

ISO 9001 is the result of what is called a voluntary consensus standards development process. Most developed countries have a unique (unique in a given country) non-profit organization that accredits voluntary consensus standards development organizations in that country. Within the United States (US), that organization is the American National Standards Institute (ANSI). ANSI and each of its parallel accrediting organizations in other countries represent those countries to ISO—the International Organization for Standardization. ISO's focus is business process standards, and its committees are made up of country representatives.

At this writing, ISO has one issued standard in the field of intellectual capital management: ISO 10688 "Brand Valuation—Requirements for Monetary Brand Valuation." And there is one additional relevant ISO standard that is still in development (as of this writing): ISO/TC 279 "Innovation Management."

In addition, one of the ANSI accredited US standards developers—LES (the Licensing Executives Society, USA and Canada)—is also active in this field. It is a professional organization of intellectual capital management experts, and it has several draft standards in various stages of development:

- Intellectual Assets in the Boardroom
- IP Protection in the Supply Chain
- IP Valuation
- IP Brokerage
- IP Licensing
- FRAND (Fair, Reasonable And Non-Discriminatory) Licensing
- IP Management for Startups

(Please note the contrast in terminology here. Most of the people leading and participating in these committees are used to the term "intellectual property or IP" and are less keen on using the term "intellectual capital." In my view, for most of these people in most of these committees, this is may be more a matter of habit than a matter of conviction. If we business-people work at it, perhaps the community will gradually move to terminology that is more easily explicable and consistent and that is more relatable to other business-people.)

My understanding is that LES's originally stated purposes for its intellectual capital management standards work are the following:

- Make good intellectual capital management and transaction practice more understandable and accessible throughout the enterprise, from the boardroom down to individual contributors
- Improve the practice of intellectual capital management and, by doing so, enhance shareholder value and mitigate litigation risk through the establishment of safe harbors
- Enhance the efficiency of and reduce the cost and time required to do intellectual capital transactions and management
- Establish expectations for how an enterprise manages and protects intellectual capital in its relationships with third parties
- Protect and preserve intellectual capital value for innovative individuals and enterprises
- Encourage investment in innovation and enhance the economic well-being of society

Today, as we have already discussed, in the world of intellectual capital management, there is regular disorder within companies and between companies. The result often is that work involving intellectual capital transactions and enterprise management of intellectual capital is sometimes inefficient and ineffective. High costs are incurred, much time is wasted, risks become elevated, pertinent business processes are error-prone and misdirected, and confusion may sometimes reign. Discussions and negotiations are more emotionally charged when intellectual capital management questions and issues are considered, and the results are less rational and determinate.

Meanwhile, as organizations dither or chase their tails, their intellectual capital dwindles in value. Standards are one way to make the management of intellectual capital more understandable and accessible throughout the enterprise. They hold the promise of reducing the disorder and ultimately of enhancing enterprise value. These are the reasons business process standards in intellectual capital management should be taken seriously by business leaders.

The reason that ISO standards and ANSI standards (standards developed by ANSI-accredited organizations) are preferable is that they are developed in a fair, balanced, due-process-driven, consensus-based way. Both organizations (ISO and ANSI) have rules by which standards need to be developed, and those rules require openness and balance across the ecosystem that will be affected by the standard. While these rules can cause standards to take a long time to be developed and revised (years, in most cases), the affected community can be assured that once ratified, the standard will reflect the perspectives of a diversity of economic actors. (Please refer to the *ANSI Essential Requirements: Due Process Requirements for American National Standards*, which is available on the ANSI web site, to examine ANSI's rules for standards development.)

An objection has been made to the scope of some of the LES draft standards mentioned above: that business process or management framework standards should only apply to one enterprise's processes, not to the processes of two or more parties working toward a possible transaction. Observers point out that ANSI has a prohibition against commercial agreements forming the basis of an ANSI standard.

My reply to these observations is that the multi-party LES standards are not commercial agreements and do not point to specific terms in commercial agreements but rather are standards that attempt to balance the reasonable expectations of each of the parties in the lead-up to a possible agreement. And yes, I will freely admit that this sort of a standard may be new in the history of business process and management framework standards. But there is good reason to break new ground here.

Market power asymmetry (which often implies financial power asymmetry) is routinely used by larger enterprises to coerce intellectual capital rights from smaller enterprises. Whether the smaller enterprises are suppliers of products and services to the larger enterprises or whether they are attempting to be paid a reasonable royalty for the larger enterprise's use of their intellectual property rights (such as patent or trademark rights), there is a chilling effect on innovation throughout the economy when larger companies (and the US government) are routinely allowed to coerce smaller entities' intellectual capital rights for free or for substantially less than the intellectual capital's value.

Standards in this area, symmetrically applied to both types of economic players—large companies (or any enterprise with asymmetrically high market power) and small companies (or any company with asymmetrically low market power)—can help to bring the interests of the parties into greater balance. And doing this can have the net effect of stimulating innovation and perhaps increasing the velocity of innovation.

After all, historically, the preponderance of innovation has come from small companies, small teams of innovators, and independent inventors. To the extent large companies are able to coerce intellectual capital rights from these innovators and deny innovators the full and reasonable financial benefits of their innovations, over time this behavior will depress innovation. And as I say, standards that address the business processes involved and that encourage symmetry in requirements and obligations between the parties in the lead-up to a negotiated agreement can help to preserve the culture of innovation upon which vibrant capitalism is based.

This line of thinking is specifically relevant to two of the standards mentioned in the list above:

- IP Licensing
- FRAND Licensing

The focus of the other standards is essentially internal to an enterprise, rather than relating to a company's interaction with its potential business partners. These latter standards are therefore more relevant to the objective of teaching the members of the enterprise how to do intellectual capital management to improve the enterprise's own strategic and operational effectiveness.

Who should participate in standards-setting in this field? All are certainly welcome, but it is the business-people who bring the most to the discussion. Yes, the lawyers make valuable contributions as well. But these are business processes, after all—not legal processes.

In any event, what we are talking about here is developing a cadre of business experts in intellectual capital management. Their role is separate and distinct from that of the lawyers functioning as lawyers. But these roles can be overlapping, and when they are, there is the possibility of conflict. As a result, we must manage the relationship between the two disciplines with care, to ensure that both cadres attend to their portions of the intellectual capital universe effectively and efficiently. This division of labor is the topic of the next chapter.

Chapter Eight:
The Lawyers

The main business of a lawyer is to take the romance, the mystery, the irony, the ambiguity out of everything he touches.

—**Antonin Scalia:** Julliard School Speech (2005)

A Very Short Story: A Godfather in the mob finds out that his book-keeper has stolen ten million bucks. This bookkeeper is deaf. So, the Godfather brings along his lawyer because he knows sign language. The Godfather asks the bookkeeper, "Where is the 10 million bucks you took from me?" The lawyer, using sign language, asks the bookkeeper where the money is. The bookkeeper signs, "I don't know what you're talking about." The lawyer tells the Godfather, "He says he doesn't know where it is." That's when the Godfather pulls out an 8-shot 357 Magnum Ruger Redhawk, points it at the bookkeeper's forehead, cocks the hammer, and says, "Ask him again." The lawyer signs to the bookkeeper, "He'll do it! He really will! Unless you tell him." The bookkeeper signs back, "Alright. The money is in a brown briefcase, buried under a big W in Santa Rosita State Park." The Godfather asks the lawyer, "Well?" The lawyer replies, "He says you don't have the guts to squeeze the trigger."

The moral of this story? Perhaps it is this: be extra careful when engaging the services of a lawyer.

I've been a member of LES (the professional society for intellectual capital management) continuously since 2003, but before that, I was a member for a few years in the middle 1990s. About a third of the members of LES are lawyers. There are a lot of patent lawyers and trademark and copyright lawyers, and there are some litigators. I worked with many of these lawyers on various LES committees and on the board of LES for a number of years, and they seem like regular people to me.

They generally know how to have a good time, and they are willing—many of them—to devote significant time, talent, and treasure to working for the common good of the profession of intellectual capital management. I have quite a few LES friends who happen to be lawyers.

Some of them are "in-house," and some of them work in law firms. Some of them are former lawyers and now identify themselves as business-people. Most of the lawyers who work as lawyers and that I would count as friends work in law firms, but not all. Almost all of the lawyers I've come to know through LES are collegial, cooperative, congenial, friendly, and generous.

And some of the lawyers I've worked with in the several operating companies I've worked for have been charming, supportive, helpful, and collaborative. In fact, the first patent lawyer with which I worked, mentored me, taught me, and helped me understand the role of business people in operating companies when it comes to what I now call intellectual capital management. And I don't think he would disagree with much of what I say here.

But this hasn't always been my experience with the "in-house" lawyers that I've worked with. In fact, working with a few lawyers in one or two of my former companies has been quite difficult, full of tension and conflict.

I bring this up because it bears upon the proposition that this small essay is designed to advance: that some companies could benefit structurally and financially (and from the perspective of risk mitigation) by establishing a business-focused intellectual capital management group with a diverse set of business management, deal-making, intellectual capital valuation, standards development, project management, alliance management, business process design, and business strategy skills. There are quite simply some intellectual property lawyers who view such a function as an encroachment on their span of control, a usurpation of their authority, and a threat to the well-being of the enterprise. As a consequence, we must talk about this.

Of course, there is good reason for the lawyers to be responsible for all matters involving the law. And they arguably may be better positioned than others to lead the design of business processes that relate directly to legal matters, such as invention disclosure/patenting processes, document marking processes and regimes, the use of nondisclosure agreements, pre-litigation and litigation activity, prosecution of registrations (i.e., patents, trademarks, and copyrights), and so forth.

Where there is a significant opportunity for ambiguity, however, is in transactions, and by transactions I mean such things as intellectual capital licensing (whether in or out), its sale or acquisition, and various sorts of collaboration relationships—such as joint ventures, joint development efforts, strategic alliances, and consortium relationships—in which intellectual capital licensing or assignment (sale and/or purchase) may be at the heart of such relationships.

Intellectual property lawyers (lawyers specializing in patent, copyright, trademark, and trade secret law) have historically been the go-to resources for all matters having to do with intellectual capital management within some operating companies. As a result, they are used to being the authority on many questions and issues having to do with intellectual capital that fall outside of the legal regime. Business leaders are used to going to them uniquely for business advice having to do with intellectual capital transactions, since few business-people seem to understand this field—the questions that should be asked and answered, reasonable and conventional negotiating behavior, intellectual capital rights valuation, and normal business and financial positions that might be taken.

Of course, one of the most important inputs to doing an informed intellectual capital transaction is the value of the intellectual capital rights that are in question. Other key inputs are answers to the following questions: what is the business objective, and what is the best way of achieving that objective? More specifically, one wants to know what sort of business relationship would work best to achieve that objective, and what the key elements of such a relationship should be.

All of these latter subjects—the business objective, the value of the intellectual capital, the form of the business and financial relationship, and key elements of that relationship—are not legal. They are one hundred percent business considerations. And so too are the identification of the intellectual capital and the intellectual capital rights that are central to the transaction.

Of course, intellectual capital can have legal protection associated with it, but identifying the intellectual capital and the intellectual capital rights that should be at play in the transaction are typically a business matter. Yes, lawyers can be helpful in figuring this out. In fact, they and the technical people are critical to tracking down all the registered intellectual capital (such as patents, trademarks, and copyrighted material). But leadership in this area is a business rather than a legal or technical function.

Of course, the intellectual property lawyers are essential to assessing the quality of the legal protections of the assets in question and in assessing whether these assets have already been licensed, whether the assets in question are in fact owned by the company, and whether the company's ability to license the assets is impaired in any way. The lawyers also can be very helpful in understanding the legal risks of taking various positions and developing certain sorts of business relationships. This is very much in their wheelhouse. And when the companies involved in the relationship are located in different countries, the lawyers will need to be doubly busy figuring out from a legal perspective how to set up any implementing agreements.

But the fact is that the business-people should have the best handle on what intellectual capital assets and rights would be needed by the company and the other party or parties to the transaction. The participation by the lawyers in this sorting out work will typically not hurt and may help. They should therefore participate but not lead, in their capacity as lawyers.

Here is where I have run into problems. Lawyers are sometimes used to leading this work, in the absence of informed business leadership. (As I say, most business leaders have not read the books and the papers, and neither have they attended the courses and conferences, nor have they had much practical and effective experience in the field of intellectual capital transactions. They simply are not aware of what the normative practices are.) And when a business-person—such as myself—actually knows how to do this work and is willing to do it and steps up to do it, this behavior is interpreted by some lawyers as stepping into their shoes. Or perhaps more precisely as stepping on their toes.

Some intellectual property lawyers take the position that they are the only ones qualified to identify the intellectual capital assets and rights associated with a particular transaction, because the protection of these assets is in some measure a construct of the law. In other words, in their minds such assets have their being and their value by virtue of the legal protections accorded them. Some intellectual property lawyers also say that business-people are not qualified to identify the relevant assets and rights, because they are not lawyers.

Further, I've heard some intellectual property lawyers try to advance the thesis that enterprise business leaders cannot have competent thoughts and conversations about intellectual capital without the assistance of intellectual property lawyers, because they are not themselves intellectual property lawyers. Some lawyers advance this notion, even though throughout the enterprise on any given day, there are thousands or tens of thousands of conversations that take place about intellectual capital, the best way to stimulate its development, the right amount to invest in it, the right amount to ask for or pay for license rights, the best (extra-legal) ways to protect intellectual capital placed in the hands of business partners and government agencies, the best way to protect third parties' intellectual capital, and the best way to price software and subscription services—which is all about pricing the use of intellectual capital in licensed products and services.

In my conversations with lawyers on this topic, I have asked whether in the case of real property that my company wants to buy or sell, I need a lawyer to tell me what that is and what rights I may need to the real property I want to buy. Should a lawyer determine what my business interests are in the purchase of real property? The usual answer is of course not. Real property is a legal construct, I reply, just as intellectual property is. But just because there are some rights that are theoretically protected by a body of law does not necessarily mean I need a lawyer at my shoulder every step of the way or that I need a lawyer to tell me what my business interests are. Yes, there are many steps in the process of doing an intellectual capital transaction that the lawyers need to be involved with, but not all, and not in a determinative business role.

And here is another conundrum: many business-people in my experience shy away from negotiating intellectual capital transactions. They regard this work as what the lawyers do. And I think they think this way because they have no familiarity themselves. They have little experience in negotiating such agreements. They haven't read the books and taken the courses on this. They don't go to conferences on this. As a consequence, they think the lawyers are better suited to negotiate such matters. (But of course, in their minds, negotiating price and terms and conditions related to hardware and engineering services transactions are a very different matter; in such cases, most business people would not for a moment consider turning over negotiations to a lawyer.)

And so, when I—a business-person—want to lead the business consulting work with the pertinent business unit in an intellectual capital transaction, sometimes the lawyers are shocked, affronted, dismayed, and perturbed. At least, this has been true of a few.

Some have regarded our roles as competitive. Some have wanted to limit my participation to valuing the intellectual capital rights in transactions and to reserve for themselves the consulting work whereby the business and technical people weigh the various approaches to a possible business relationship. When I have pointed out that in order to weigh these different approaches in an informed way, we may often have to run various valuation scenarios to get to an answer, I have been greeted with blank stares. By attempting to reserve the initial relationship assessment role for themselves—without any quantitative analysis—they in effect reduce the team's ability to appreciate fully the financial implications of the alternatives they should reasonably consider.

So, when setting up an intellectual capital management function, there ought to be clarity around the roles of the lawyers and the business-people. I like the way the relationship works in the world of mergers and acquisitions (M&A). The business people specializing in M&A do the valuation, work with the investment bankers, get alignment with the relevant business unit that may benefit from the transaction, work out with that business unit the strategic and financial benefits, assemble the team, lead the team, and lead the negotiations.

In M&A transactions, the lawyers are responsible for the implementing agreements. There is discussion between the lawyers and M&A people on many issues, but it's clear that the lawyers lead when it comes to the risk management terms, while the business-people lead when it comes to the value-driving terms. As I say, the business people—the M&A business specialists—have responsibility for organizing the team, inventorying the assets, leading the negotiations, and finally deciding what the business and financial arrangement—balancing all of the risks and equities—should look like, with significant input from the relevant business unit, finance, the company's senior leadership, and board of directors.

Placing business leadership for intellectual capital transactions in the hands of the lawyers robs deal teams of a quantitative understanding of the different alternatives and may encourage a market-power-based, bluff-and-bluster, brinksmanship type of discussion and negotiation. Such negotiations can be uninformed by valuation methodologies and valuation consensus. One wants to know what the minimum list of intellectual capital and intellectual capital rights would be to meet the needs of the parties, and agreement in this area is difficult to achieve without some sense of the value of the intellectual capital rights being discussed.

Licensing transactions should be good for both the licensor and the licensee (or assignor and assignee). The parties should be willing and perhaps even anxious to reach an agreement where both benefit to a reasonable degree. How do people understand whether what they are asking for is unreasonable from the other party's perspective and from the perspective of market comparables? Very often, it is helpful to spell out the value of the intellectual capital rights from the perspective of each party so that balance in the parties' financial interests can be achieved.

When I say "value," I'm specifically not talking about price. Anyone can come up with a price arbitrarily. A price can come from anywhere for any reason. But we're not considering that here. What we are trying to do is to determine—given industry norms and standards in the field of intellectual capital rights valuation—an objective and reasonable assessment of the value of the intellectual capital rights in question. We are seeking the perspective of an intellectual capital rights valuation expert operating independent of both parties to the transaction.

Some lawyers are not used to this. So too with some business-people. Both can be exceptionally uncomfortable with rigorous discussions concerning intellectual capital value. Both groups are used to price discussions and negotiations, but they are unfamiliar with value discussions and negotiations. And because they are uncomfortable, some business-people and some lawyers would prefer not to have them.

Senior business leaders are often able to take more informed positions in their negotiations around the licensing of intellectual capital rights when they have a sense of the value of the rights being discussed. There are alternative ways to realize intellectual capital value, but exploration of these alternatives is closed to the business people when value is not a key consideration in internal decision-making, negotiations, and deal-making.

In conclusion, negative consequences accrue to companies who confuse the roles of the intellectual property lawyers and the business-people and when the business people have little experience with value-based intellectual capital transaction analysis and strategy. Why can't we have clarity in the roles, responsibility, and authority in intellectual capital rights transactions and in intellectual capital rights management? We can. We simply have to set out the guidelines and educate both the lawyers and the business-people, ensuring that they have the knowledge and skill and guidance to play their different roles well.

But—one might ask—what should one do to educate the organization more broadly on how to manage intellectual capital better? We take up this question in the next chapter.

Chapter Nine:

Educating the Company

The value of a business is a function of how well the financial capital and the intellectual capital are managed by the human capital. You'd better get the human capital part right.

—**Dave Bookbinder:** *The NEW ROI*

The basic economic resource, the means of production, is no longer capital, natural resources, or labor, but knowledge. Value is now created by "productivity" and "innovation," both applications of knowledge to work.

—**Peter Drucker:** *Post Capitalist Society*

A Very Short Story: "Bye, Bye, Blackboard" is the 193rd and final animated cartoon short in the original Woody Woodpecker series. In it, Woody is a student in Mrs. Meany's class. He arrives late to school, along with his dog, Alfie. Mrs. Meany kicks Alfie out, but he bites Mrs. Meany in the caboose. Woody commits mayhem and consequently must stand in the corner under a dunce cap. Woody rings the school bell, indicating recess. Then Mrs. Meany chases him and ends up spanking him for his misdeeds.

The moral of this story? Perhaps it is this: for some of us, with a penchant for misbehaving, learning can be painful and a trial for everyone around us. (I'm speaking from personal experience, here.)

Introduction

Ignorance can be a pretty stubborn thing. And it can be fierce, too, like a grizzly bear into whose territory one has inadvertently stepped. Grizzlies can be fast when they like, chasing down the hapless interloper at 30 miles per hour.

I recall a conversation between me, my manager, and a senior company executive concerning some intellectual capital valuation and consulting work my office had done for this executive and his team. My manager asked him if he wouldn't mind putting in a good word for me and my team with his leader and letting his leader know that we had helped save the company a significant amount of money through the work we had done.

His reply tells us volumes about the difficulty of helping business leaders understand and become proficient at intellectual capital management. He said something like the following: you expect me to tell my leader that I was too ignorant to figure out that I was just about to sign a deal in which I would unnecessarily transfer millions of dollars in intellectual capital rights? And that I needed Bill and his team to help me understand what I was doing?

Now, one part of me wanted to say to this guy (a guy who has done wonderful things for the company and for whom I have a great deal of respect) that he doesn't expect to be proficient in power supply design without spending years and years studying and doing power supply designs. Neither does he expect to become an expert in currency hedging by taking a five-week course over the internet. So why would he expect to understand that his business partner was asking him to sign over millions of dollars in intellectual capital value, when his business partner only had a vague notion of what he was doing, himself?

The main issue for many companies that find themselves in the middle of the knowledge economy is that their business leaders were educated in a business management curriculum that was crafted mainly on a mid-20th century theory of the firm. The firm that they were educated to manage had as its major assets financial capital, access to financial markets, natural resources, physical property, channels to market, and labor. Even today, business leaders are often not taught by their business schools to manage businesses in which 60-90 percent of the firm's assets are intangible. Some are not taught about intellectual capital value and about strategies for the optimal preservation and extraction of intellectual capital value. They are often not taught about how to accelerate the velocity of high-quality, focused innovation in their enterprises or to understand what "high quality" innovation looks like.

And because of this, intellectual capital is invisible to some business leaders or, if visible to them, such leaders may have a hard time knowing what they are looking at—what the intellectual capital actually is and what its significance is. I'm reminded of a skit on a *Saturday Night Live* show back when the Earth's crust was still cooling. Steve Martin and Bill Murray wonder what something is that they keep looking at, off camera.

Steve Martin arrives on stage alone in a green-patterned Hawaiian shirt and shorts, with a camera in his hand. "What in the *hell* is that?" he asks. He squints and then says, "What in the hell *is* that?"

Steve Martin then asks several other questions, pausing between each one: "What's that dang thing doing here?" "How did that get here?" "What the *hell* is that?" "What the *hell* is that?" "How did that dang deal get here?" "Hey, come over here and look at this deal!"

Bill Murray comes onto camera, making the crooked clown mouth he sometimes made in those days, and says, "What the hell is that?"

Then Steve Martin says, "I don't know what the hell that is!"

Bill Murray replies, "What in the hell *is that?*"

Steve Martin warns, "Hey, you kids, get away from there!"

Bill Murray joins him, saying, "I wouldn't rest on that thing!"

Steve Martin: "Don't put your lips on it!"

Bill Murray: "What in the hell *is* this?"

Steve Martin: "Well, get a photo of me with it, anyway."

He goes off camera, and Bill Murray says, "Be careful with that thing!"

Bill Murray snaps the photo, and Steve Martin comes back onto camera.

Bill Murray: "Oh, I know what that is."

Steve Martin: *"Well, what the **hell** is it?"*

Bill Murray: "What the hell is that thing, anyways?"

Steve Martin: "I don't even care what it is. ***What the hell is it?***"

Bill Murray: "I don't know what the hell that thing is."

Steve Martin: "Oh, now I know what it is."

Bill Murray: "Oh, yeah."

As they walk off camera, Steve Martin says, *"What the **hell** was it?"*

What to do? We need to make the enterprise's intellectual capital visible and its significance understandable to people. We have to put policies and processes in place that will motivate people to identify the firm's intellectual capital. We must construct required courses to teach these policies and processes because without required courses (computer-based modules, for example), the business-people won't activate them. (They will be merely additional files taking up space on the company's servers.) Then we have to audit these policies and processes routinely to ensure that the business-people have a clear understanding of "what is in it for me?" If they are managing the intellectual capital correctly, they pass their audits. Passing an audit is a very positive motivator.

Is this draconian or unnecessarily punitive? Not at all. If a company's leadership is committed to changing the way people in the company think about and behave regarding intellectual capital, these can be very effective steps.

Of course, the avoidance of intellectual capital value loss or the gain of value through intellectual capital transactions done well should be sufficient motivators, but they sometimes are not. Sometimes, the business-person would rather do the job given him in the manner he has been taught to do that job or how he has historically been expected to do that job and would not like to make any significant changes to it. Some people do not like learning new things, and people sometimes get anxious when expectations change or increase. This is especially so when there is a great deal to learn and to master.

Sometimes the individual and organizational goals and rewards are off-kilter. Sometimes intellectual capital rights transactions are not considered.

But one does need to show the business-people what they can accomplish financially by making the change we are discussing. We do need to show that a good deal of money can be saved and made by managing intellectual capital well.

We also need courses—and I'm not talking necessarily about full-blown college or graduate school type courses, with papers and exams—that will help business-people see the intellectual capital and understand its value. We need to present case studies that illustrate best practices through good examples. We need to put the business-people into teams that sift through the case studies to find the intellectual capital bits and pieces. We need to illustrate the value of the intellectual capital with business cases, showing what can go haywire and what can go well. We need to show the business-people what the practices are that lead to negative outcomes and to positive outcomes. And finally we need to show the business-people the importance of quantitative analysis in assessing business alternatives.

The Human and Organizational Reality

A company's most senior leaders are potentially the most enthusiastic champions for managing intellectual capital well. Since they are ultimately responsible for the enterprise's financial performance, they should be the most interested in learning about this field and in encouraging their employees to learn about it as well. However, there are paradoxes here. One of them is that the more senior the business leader, the more that leader has been encouraged—through promotions and pay raises and the good opinion of his colleagues and managers—to think that he has mastered the knowledge and skills required to manage all relevant assets of his corner of the company.

But of course, this may not be the case. The typical senior leader in a 21st century U.S. company will sometimes not have a thorough understanding of intellectual capital, what managing it well looks like, what the relevant metrics are regarding its management, how to use it to advantage in crafting new business models, how to negotiate business relationships in which it is central, how to assess its value when rights to it are being discussed, how to assess the strength of any legal protections and their relevance to its value, how to manage supply chains to reduce the risk of catastrophic intellectual capital loss, how to assess the impacts to the business that adopting software-centric and data-centric business models will have, and so forth. Like the leader I referred to above, senior business-people are sometimes threatened by their own ignorance. It is not easy for a senior leader to admit that there is a significant field of knowledge and skill relevant to the optimal management of the firm with which he is not familiar.

People have difficulty owning up to their own ignorance and to doing something about it. (I know I do.) This is the central paradox in intellectual capital management today. And it isn't limited to senior leaders in companies. It exists throughout many companies today and throughout many business schools. I've spoken with many business school professors and deans and administrators. They do not have the academic framework for thinking about and understanding the firm from this perspective, from the perspective of needing actively to manage most of the firm's structural capital assets with the same rigor as the firm's tangible assets.

I have worked principally in industrial, aerospace, and defense electronics companies, and people there have found it difficult to change the way they think about business models and intellectual capital generally. In a number of the companies I've worked for, the attitude has been to provide support to the development of the company's knowledge and competency in this new area but to do so slowly. Yes, there has been a recognition of the contribution experts in the field can make, but acceptance has been slow.

There has been a reluctance on the part of some finance people to agree that they may not be knowledgeable and skilled in intellectual capital valuation, even though they have received no instruction in this relatively arcane field. Sometimes, they have felt that they are qualified to do intellectual capital valuation because of their familiarity with enterprise business valuation approaches and because of their experience with general financial analysis and net present value analysis.

For example, I remember someone in a finance organization that, with poise and grace, argued to apply a fixed 5 percent royalty to all arms-length, cross-jurisdictional intra-company intellectual capital licensing transactions—transfer pricing situations. Of course, this approach ignores the differential relative value of one bundle of intellectual capital rights versus another in different use scenarios, varying product and service economics situations, and competitive environments. The assumption here is that all intellectual capital has the same relative value, no matter the varying facts of the application. Of course, this is fallacious.

It is one of the first things one learns in the study of intellectual capital valuation—that one approach or one bottom-line answer to all intellectual capital valuation scenarios won't work. The approach selected must be suited to the facts of the case to have any hope of being defensible and useful.

From time to time, I've received a defensive response from some people in the contracts and subcontracts organizations—the organizations charged with developing and negotiating intellectual capital licensing and purchase or sale agreements for intellectual capital. Some in these organizations have tried to deflect responsibility for identifying the intellectual capital and the associated rights in the transactions in which they are involved. I've been told that the people we should really be focusing on with our education and training are the program managers, product line managers, business developers, and account managers that typically lead the front end of any new business pursuits or business relationships.

When I point out that the contracts and subcontracts managers are responsible for the language in the contractual agreements and that this language refers to specific intellectual capital assets and particular rights to these assets, I am sometimes told that the contracts and subcontracts folks are typically not conceptually involved. They have not been involved in the design of the deal but are rather brought in later on, after the basic outlines of the relationship have been discussed and agreed to by the business leaders.

From time to time, the thesis of a few of the contracts and subcontracts leaders—and some of the individual contributors as well—seems to be that they are involved with but are not responsible for the company's intellectual capital transactions; therefore, they should not have to understand intellectual capital matters too deeply. They should not be held uniquely responsible for the agreements they are involved with writing and negotiating, from the perspective of really understanding the intellectual capital rights involved.

What I sometimes have heard from some people in the contracts and subcontracts organizations in the various companies for which I have worked is that the program managers, product line managers, business developers, and account managers should be the experts in intellectual capital matters. Further, some have counseled me that they are not the decision makers when we craft deals with our customers, suppliers, co-development partners (frenemies, as some people call them), and government agencies; so, they (the contracts and subcontracts managers) should not be expected to know the details of the deal. In fact, from time to time, I have gotten the distinct impression that some contracts and subcontracts people are in a full sprint away from knowing too much about intellectual capital transactions, how to spot intellectual capital and its associated rights in a larger transaction, or even how to structure a license agreement.

Similarly, when I have spoken with some pricing leaders in some of my former employers, I've also received deflective responses. I've been told that their pricing people had been educated in how to price engineering services and hardware, but intellectual capital, software, software as a service, and information and data as a service were not in their repertoire. Besides, they didn't see these kinds of transactions, they said.

But truth be told, some didn't ask the sorts of questions of the program managers, business developers, account managers, and product line managers that would get at whether any of these sorts of things were in fact embedded in the transactions they priced. And without the pricing people asking a bunch of questions about this sort of thing, intellectual capital rights can be given away without anyone having any idea that this is happening. In other words, the intellectual capital embedded in hardware and engineering services transactions can be invisible to the pricing people, along with everyone else.

Again, the metaphor of the footrace comes to mind, a footrace with a 30-mile-per-hour grizzly bear. How can a company operating in a knowledge economy expect to stay in business with these attitudes? How can it expect to know what it is doing? How can it expect to know the volume or value of the intellectual capital rights it is transferring to its customers, suppliers, co-development partners, and relevant government agencies? How can it understand how its own business model may be changing underneath its feet?

Finally, when I have proposed that we educate the program managers, product line managers, business developers, and account managers on what intellectual capital is, why rights to it are valuable, how to spot it, how to develop strategies around how to transact it, and so forth, in some companies I have sometimes been greeted with an adamantine "No!"

The reason given is that these business-people are too busy, too fully occupied, too burdened by other educational assignments, too overwhelmed by all the subjects they are required to master and tasks they need to perform. The position their leadership has sometimes taken is that there is no way that these business-people should or could be expected to become experts in intellectual capital management and intellectual capital licensing transactions.

But little-to-no-education for business leaders is not an adequate approach in a company whose intellectual capital represents 60-90 percent of its equity value and in a business environment characterized by the following:

- Customers, suppliers, co-development partners, and government agencies who routinely try to coerce intellectual capital rights away from the company and to pay nothing or next to nothing for those rights
- The need to place sensitive, highly valuable intellectual capital into the hands of customers, suppliers, co-development partners, and government agencies who are in emerging markets or who have little in the way of policy, process, access control, auditing, education, and management attention on the way in which they care for business partners' intellectual capital
- Rapid business model change in the direction of software, information, and access services (such as access to networks or information or software)
- The need to price new intangible products, services, and enabling capabilities (such as tools, environments, and frameworks) in the areas of software, information, and access

Intellectual Capital Management Curriculum for Business-People

It is nerve-wracking to have to stand up in front of senior company leaders who are two or three levels above one's pay grade and talk about the intellectual capital issues, value, strategy, rights, pricing structure, key licensing terms and risks, strength of the legal protections, risk of reverse engineering, selected discount rate, assumed cost of goods sold, reasonable split of the profits between licensor and licensee or joint owners, and so forth, in a particular transaction. It's nerve-wracking because one sometimes has limited knowledge of these subjects, if one is a typical program manager, product line manager, business developer, or account manager. Some of these concepts are foreign to many business-people with whom I have worked.

On the other hand, if a program manager is bringing forward an intellectual capital transaction for pricing approval, he had better understand what he is doing well enough to do it well. Yes, he will want to rely on a variety of experts on his team: engineering, for example, legal, contracts, pricing, accounting, manufacturing, and so forth. And yes, one of the experts can even be from the discipline of intellectual capital management. However, the program manager will need to speak the language of intellectual capital well enough to speak in an informed and insightful way about the intellectual capital matters at hand, at least well enough to answer the reasonable questions of leadership in a bid or pricing review. Well enough to teach his leadership about key intellectual capital management concepts related to the transaction at hand.

What does such a person need to know to put together a competent and an effective presentation on an intellectual capital transaction or a proposed strategic relationship with a business partner that will crucially involve intellectual capital rights? He'll need to know something (not necessarily a lot and certainly not everything) about the following:

- The company's intellectual capital transaction policy and process
- The company's delegation of authority for pricing intellectual capital rights
- Intellectual capital valuation and financial analysis techniques
    - Includes a consideration of the concepts of value, cost, and price
- Conventional payment structures in intellectual capital licensing and joint ownership agreements
- Value-driving terms in intellectual capital agreements
- How to spot intellectual capital items or conveyances
- How to divide up intellectual capital rights
- Negotiation of intellectual capital licenses and assignments
    - The use of valuation analysis and term sheets
- Strategic relationships: development of intellectual capital rights arrangements in the case of multi-party contributions

Each of the above bulleted items could be a learning module. If each is designed as an instructor-led learning experience, with exercises where appropriate, the modules could vary from one to three hours. Altogether, to deliver enough knowledge and understanding for business-people who are not intellectual capital management specialists to manage intellectual capital transactions, the scope of all these modules should probably span a several-day learning experience. I wouldn't plan to deliver all the modules together over that period. It would be too much information to absorb, for most people. Rather, I would space deliveries out over the span of a few weeks or months, with reading assigned in between sessions.

Perhaps this education isn't for everyone. Perhaps it should be assigned on an as-needed basis. For example, certain business-people can be identified as the go-to people to handle intellectual capital intensive transactions and business relationships.

There should be refresher courses delivered on a regular basis following the initial education to remind and reinforce the initial learning. In these sessions, students should be encouraged to bring real world problems and examples to class as business cases to examine and discuss. A half-day refresher periodically would not be over-kill for this purpose. Remember, what we are doing here is opening the eyes of some (perhaps many) business people to a world that is mostly invisible to them. We are teaching them a language they largely do not know. It often takes quite a bit of work to see the world of intellectual capital and see it whole and to master the key areas of knowledge sufficiently to manage a company's considerably valuable intellectual capital store.

Intellectual Capital Management Curriculum for Contracts and Subcontracts People

What do the contracts and subcontracts people need to know about intellectual capital management to do their jobs well? Like the businesspeople, they need to know the following:

- The company's intellectual capital transaction policy and process
- The company's delegation of authority for pricing intellectual capital rights

But they also need to understand how to structure agreements and how to negotiate agreements in which intellectual capital ownership and license rights play a significant role. Specifically, they need to become expert in developing the term sheet, which contains the key elements of such agreements. The term sheet can contain both of the following:

- Value driving (business and financial) terms
- Risk management terms

To be effective, the term sheet should focus on the key business terms. It is used to obtain internal alignment as to what the contemplated relationship and implementing agreement will actually look like. And it is used to obtain alignment between and among the parties to the relationship.

Of course, the contracts and subcontracts people will need to work with the transaction lead, business developer, the intellectual property attorney, intellectual capital management/valuation person, pricing person, and the technologists (for example) to sort out what the intellectual capital is and what the rights are that need to be addressed in the term sheet. Through the process of putting together a term sheet, the deal team will sort out what the business strategy is for the contemplated relationship. And they will sort out what they actually will want approval to do and why.

Part of the process entails an assessment of the intellectual capital in question—ownership rights, license rights that are available, and legal protections for the intellectual capital. The contracts and subcontracts people, along with the lawyer and others on the team, will need to assess the company's ability to do the contemplated transaction, given other related transactions it might have already done. Relevant legal protections (the status of any pertinent patents, copyrights, trademarks, and trade secrets) will also need to be weighed, since they may have a bearing on the value of the intellectual capital rights that the team contemplates.

The contracts and subcontracts people are key to making all this happen. They play the role of Socratic questioner, leading the team in the development of the term sheet, which contains concepts that should eventually find their way into the agreement. The term sheet is the framework that the relationship will rest on.

Socrates was professionally ignorant. His role was to help others discover what they already knew and to discover new knowledge. This is the role of the contracts and subcontracts person. Learning to do this well is best accomplished through practice, through the study of relevant business cases, and through mentoring.

Text books on licensing and on the use of term sheets are widely available, and courses on licensing and on the use of term sheets are available through LES.

Intellectual Capital Management Curriculum for Pricing People

Intellectual capital valuation is an important way the company makes its intellectual capital visible to itself. So, the function of intellectual capital valuation is an important one.

Pricing people in the companies I've been involved with typically are responsible for pricing a wide variety of hardware-based and engineering-services-based products and services. Business developers will also be involved in pricing products and services, including software, information, and access-based products and services.

Neither group has usually received any education in valuing intellectual capital rights.

Pricing of hardware and engineering services is often reduced to an assessment of the recurring cost with appropriate amortization of the incremental investment required to tailor the offering, plus overheads and profit added as percentages on top of all this. But this method does not work well with intellectual capital valuation or valuation of software, information, and access services. In other words, the valuation of technology and proprietary information and the valuation of software, information, and access services share the characteristic of requiring a value-based pricing approach rather than a recurring-cost-based pricing approach.

Pricing people—whether pricing intellectual capital rights relating to technology, know-how, and proprietary information or whether pricing software, information, and access services—will need to learn how to do intellectual capital valuation and value-based pricing to provide useful guidance to business leaders in this important area.

What do the pricing people need to know about intellectual capital to do their jobs well? Like the business-people and the contracts and subcontracts people, they need to know the following:

- The company's intellectual capital transaction policy and process
- The company's delegation of authority for pricing intellectual capital transactions

But they also need to know something about how specifically to value intellectual capital rights. Depending on their role in the company, they may need to know how to do so in scenarios that are repeated with some frequency. In other words, they may not need to be intellectual capital valuation experts, but they should be educated by the company's intellectual capital valuation experts to understand some of the salient methods of valuation and how to apply those methods on a scenario-driven basis.

Each company's licensing scenarios will be somewhat different. This means that customized education should be developed around these repeated scenarios.

This way, experts in intellectual capital management and valuation can delegate this role for a substantial percentage of the transactions being done in the company, without requiring that the company hire an army of specialists in this important area.

I won't go into the details here, since there are several quite helpful text books available in this area, and relevant courses are available through LES. (Please see Chapter 15.)

Intellectual Capital Management Curriculum for the Lawyers

Like the other groups mentioned above, the lawyers will need to understand the following:

- The company's intellectual capital transaction policy and process
- The company's delegation of authority for pricing intellectual capital transactions

It's quite likely that the lawyers will need to review the above policies and procedures as they are being formulated and revised so that their roles and responsibilities versus the contracts and subcontracts people and versus the intellectual capital management experts are clearly articulated. While a formal curriculum for the lawyers in the above areas is likely not required, review and sign-off would be.

But this leaves the question of education in value, cost, and price. I've encountered many in the organization—including the lawyers—who become confused about these concepts, thinking that they have a handle on them (when they don't) and can guide enterprise teams in this important area (when they shouldn't). A short instructor-led course on this topic for the lawyers would, therefore, probably make some sense.

So, what is the difference between value, cost, and price? We take up this seemingly simple question briefly in the next chapter.

Chapter Ten:

Value, Cost, and Price

Price is what you pay. Value is what you get.
—**Warren Buffett:** *Berkshire Hathaway*
2008 Annual Report

A Very Short Story: In the movie, *It's a Mad Mad Mad Mad World*, several people watch as a thief accidentally drives off the road ("sailing right out there"), crashes down an embankment, and dies. The witnesses are following in three cars and a truck. There are eight people in these vehicles. Smiler Grogan—just released from prison and the man who has wrecked the car—reveals, as he literally kicks the bucket, that he has buried $350,000 in stolen money under "a big W" in Santa Rosita State Park, before being incarcerated for many years. This is 1963; so, $350,000 is big money. The four male drivers of the vehicles plus one male companion run down to Smiler to render assistance and hear his dying words. Later, up the hill, by the side of the road, as the group of eight (five males and three females) discusses what to do next, there's a value discussion:

- Mrs. Marcus: "What's this 'fair shares' for everybody?"
- Melville: "We arrived in four vehicles. I think we should split it up in four quarters."
- Ding: "Four quarters? What are you talking about? Quarters? You mean, you three each get a quarter, and Benjy and I have to split a quarter?
- Russell: "That's right. That's right."
- Benjy: "What are you trying to pull?"
- Melville: "Seems fair enough to me."
- Ding: "Naturally, it's fair to you.
- Benjy: "It just cheats us. That's all."
- Ding: "$350,000 divided by four is…let's say, $87,500."
- Russell: "That's what it is."
- Ding: "The three of you get $87,500, and Benjy and I have to split."
- Benjy: "There was five of us down at the wreck. We should split it five ways."
- Russell: "He's right. We should split it five ways."

- Melville: "I'm perfectly willing to discuss it in a five-way manner. Now we can discuss it in a five-way manner, five shares...each share would be $70,000..."
- Lenny: "$70,000? Holy mackerel! You realize how many loads I'd have to haul from Modesto to Yuma ..."
- Mrs. Marcus: "You're overlooking one thing."
- Russell: "Yeah. We're overlooking one little thing."
- Ding: "What little thing?"
- Russell: "Yeah. What little thing?"
- Mrs. Marcus: "We can all count, can't we? There were eight of us there."
- Russell: "She's right. There were eight of us there."
- Melville: "Well, speaking for my wife and myself, we'd be just as happy..."
- Ding: "You'd be just as happy with two eights instead of a quarter? That's awfully big of you."
- Lennie: "Wait a minute. Hold it. Hold it. Let's put it back the way it was before. Either one quarter for each car, including the van, or one fifth for each guy."
- Russell: "Yeah, one quarter for each car or one fifth for each guy."

The moral of this story? Perhaps it is this: value calculations cannot only be emotional; they can be emotional in proportion to what's at stake. And of course, emotion can distort one's perception of intellectual capital reality, creating a mad, mad, mad, mad world, so to say.

Introduction

To be clear, what I mean by "intellectual capital rights value" is the price a prospective licensee should be willing to pay for a specific bundle of intellectual capital rights given the particular facts of the transaction and the known facts and characteristics and outcomes of similar transactions. What I mean by "intellectual capital rights price" is the offered price or the negotiated price for intellectual capital rights. Only one of the important inputs to the pricing decision is the intellectual capital rights value. What I mean by "intellectual capital rights cost" is one or the other of the following: (1) the historical cost to the potential licensor to develop the intellectual capital bundle in question or (2) the cost that would be incurred by the potential licensee to develop a replacement intellectual capital bundle.

Discussion

As I say, there are many articles and books that treat the subject of intellectual capital rights valuation. Some are boring. Others are entertaining. Some are full of conventional wisdom, while others are innovative. I have no intention of re-plowing any of that ground here. But for business leaders interested in developing an intellectual capital management discipline in their companies, there are a few important points that I should make.

First, at the heart of enterprise intellectual capital management there should be an expert-level understanding of intellectual capital value. An expert intellectual capital valuation function within the company should be provided through consulting services to the organization. Developing and maintaining a cadre of experts in this area is an important element in being able to provide a credible value-based input to pricing of intellectual capital rights and prioritization of various legal and business process protection measures to be applied to particular intellectual capital bundles.

Second, a guide should be developed for people making investment decisions and especially for people involved with pricing intellectual capital rights—particularly for people pricing software, information, and access services. This guide should be based on the desired ratio between profits and discretionary technology investments. At the corporate level, one can look at a company's R&D expense and operating profit in a given year. For example, Microsoft's R&D expense for 2018 was $14.7B, while its operating profit was $35.058B. Its ratio of profits to R&D investment was therefore 2.38.

If a company's stock price is an acceptable multiple of its earnings, the operating profits/R&D investments ratio should be maintained. If management wants to expand the price/earnings multiple, the ratio should be increased (along with other financial performance attributes, such as revenue growth rate, for example). Pretty simple. But in some industries, simple guides like this one are hard to find. Such a guide can be a quick check on investment and pricing decisions, outside of the intellectual capital valuation assessment. In other words, such a guide is not useful as a valuation approach, but it can be a useful check on pricing of intellectual capital rights, in a corporate culture that has a tendency to want to underprice such rights when licensing out.

Third, in an industry like aerospace and defense, one's customers, suppliers, co-development partners, and government agencies sometimes overreach. In other words, such business partners look for opportunities to obtain ownership-like rights or certainly more than commercially-usual rights to a company's intellectual capital for free or certainly for substantially less than its value. Having a sense of the company's ratio between its operating profit and its R&D spend can help give the deal team and the pricing authority a point of departure for evaluating customer requests for ownership-like intellectual capital rights. Of course, a particular bundle of intellectual capital rights may turn out to be worth a great deal more than this ratio suggests, but a deal team should be reluctant to conclude that the price of those requested (or demanded) rights should be substantially less.

Further, one must keep in mind when using such a guide that the true R&D cost for an intellectual capital rights bundle likely needs to be calculated over years and in some cases over many years.

Fourth, intellectual capital valuation—as applied to intangible products and services, in particular—can be hard when the economic value to the licensee cannot be reliably calculated because the relevant facts are not known or are not knowable. And it can be hard when there are no relevant comparables or when the comparables are arguably not comparable enough. More often than not, the intellectual capital valuation expert finds himself in one or the other or both of these two circumstances. In such cases, focus groups, surveys, and auctions may be considered, as well as an analysis of the potential licensee's best alternative to a negotiated agreement (or BATNA). An additional alternative that could be considered is a special relationship with a customer who will cooperate by providing the needed financial benefit data in return for privileged pricing. In any case, the value of the intellectual capital rights cannot be any higher than the potential licensee's BATNA. As a result, valuations generally should be "BATNA-constrained."

Fifth, a potential licensee's BATNA may be its risk-adjusted cost to develop an acceptable alternative. (Here, the concept "risk-adjusted" can be important.) Complicating this consideration, and increasing the risk, is that sometimes the potential licensee does not have the human capital—the know-how—needed to develop a replacement for the intellectual capital bundle in question. And this potential licensee may not ever be able to assemble the human capital and other essential enabling structural capital for developing an acceptable alternative. In esoteric technology areas, this fact pattern is not unusual.

Sixth, price must take into consideration all of the relevant equities. The intellectual capital rights valuation is only one of these relevant equities.

Seventh, a proposed price can be whimsical, as if whispered into the ear of a business development person by a being from Mars. Value—as John Cleese used to say—is something completely different.

Eighth, historical cost is generally less than completely relevant. One doesn't invest in intellectual capital at some risk—sometimes at great risk—merely to win back what one has invested. One wants a fair, risk-adjusted return on one's investments. The risk adjustment in the analysis can therefore be critical to understanding the value of the intellectual capital, from the investor's perspective. On the other hand, the licensee may not find any of this pertinent, since the cost and risk of development today may be dramatically less than the risk-adjusted historic cost. And the discount on the risk and cost may overwhelm any calculation of opportunity costs—the costs associated with the delay introduced by having to develop surrogate intellectual capital.

Ninth, when a licensing "opportunity" diminishes rather than increases the financial performance of the licensor, the value calculation naturally veers quite dramatically toward lost profits.

Tenth, the cost of a negative honeymoon experience with a woodpecker may not necessarily mean that such an experience has or had or may have a negative value, over the long-term. Remember the story of Walter and Gracie Lantz, principals in the Walter Lantz Production Company. On their honeymoon, a woodpecker kept them awake at night and drilled holes into the roof of their rental cabin, through which the rain inexorably came, robbing them of both comfort and pleasure. This robbery certainly resulted in a cost that one could calculate. But later, once the bird was properly reimagined (or some might say, "understood"), Walter's and Gracie's livelihoods were significantly enhanced by the licensing of Woody Woodpecker cartoons. The paradoxical Woody became for them—and perhaps for some of the rest of us—a pearl of great value. (Or at least a glass marble of childish delight.)

Eleventh, *et cetera*.

But how does one know that all this arcane knowledge, education, and skill around value, cost, and price and intellectual capital management, generally, actually benefit a company? How does one track down whether the light is worth the candle? We discuss these questions in our next chapter.

Chapter Eleven:

Metrics

I often say that when you can measure what you are speaking about, and Express it in numbers, you know something about it; but when you cannot Express it in numbers, your knowledge is of a meagre and unsatisfactory Kind; it may be the beginning of knowledge, but you have scarcely, in your Thoughts, advanced to the stage of science, whatever the matter may be.
—**Lord Kelvin:** May 3, 1883 lecture:
"Electrical Units of Measurement" (*Popular Lectures*, Vol. 1, page 73)

What's measured improves.
—**Peter Drucker:** Source unknown

A Very Short Story: Fred Schwed Jr.'s classic investment book, *Where Are the Customers' Yachts?* contains the following pithy couple of paragraphs: "In 1929 there was a luxurious club car which ran each week-day morning into the Pennsylvania Station. When the train stopped, the assorted millionaires who had been playing bridge, reading the paper, and comparing their fortunes, filed out of the front end of the car. Near the door there was placed a silver bowl with a quantity of nickels in it. Those who needed a nickel in change for the subway ride downtown took one. They were not expected to put anything back in exchange; this was not money—it was one of those minor conveniences like a quill toothpick for which nothing is charged. It was only five cents.

"There have been many explanations of the sudden debacle of October 1929. The explanation I prefer is that the eye of Jehovah, a wrathful god, happened to chance in October on that bowl. In sudden understandable annoyance, Jehovah kicked over the financial structure of the United States, and thus saw to it that the bowl of free nickels disappeared forever."

The moral of this story? Perhaps it is this: if business leaders continue counting intellectual capital as having little value and managing it in an *ad hoc* way, Jehovah may consequently bring their companies burning down.

As one begins to think about implementing a systematic approach to intellectual capital management, one important area that should be carefully considered is metrics. Why collect metrics at all, one might ask. Of course, the notion is to measure something if you want to understand it and if you want to improve it. You want to know whether you are getting better or worse or whether what you are doing is making no difference.

At the enterprise and profit-and-loss-center level, there are a couple of areas that come immediately to mind. First, you could count the number of dollars coming in from out-licensing. In the areas of technology, patent, and trademark licensing, this may be interesting but perhaps not significant. If your enterprise doesn't have a business model that depends strategically on licensing of these kinds, then perhaps counting the dollars in royalties in this area would not be useful.

But if your business model is changing and you are becoming more software-centric, more information-centric, and/or more subscription-and-services-centric in your offerings, it may make sense to split out intangible product/service licensing revenues. Of course, you want to understand the rate of business model change, and you want to understand your profitability in the different parts of your business: hardware, engineering services, and intellectual capital (software, information, and access) licensing, for example. Under these circumstances, counting royalties in this area may make a great deal of sense.

Second, you could keep track of the ratio of price to value. If your valuation work is spot on and your price consistent with the calculated value, and the market accepts your pricing, you would have a ratio of 1:1. If you are consistently pricing your rights—whether technology, patent, or trademark rights or software, information, or access rights—at one half of the value estimate, the price-to-value ratio would of course be 1:2. That might tell you that you are consistently underpricing your intellectual capital rights, or it might tell you that you are consistently over-valuing your intellectual capital, or it might be telling you a little bit of both. Investigation and assessment would be in order here, and adjustments may need to be made.

If the metrics you are collecting are significantly higher than 1:1, you also might have some work to do. In fact, what I've observed in the aerospace and defense industry is that people are shy about negotiating intellectual capital value. They would sooner price intellectual capital rights at zero dollars than have a negotiation on price that is tied to a calculated value. I almost get the feeling that people in some aerospace and defense companies have the attitude that they should keep their customers and suppliers happy at any cost, and that entails giving customers and suppliers ownership-like rights to company intellectual capital for nothing or next to nothing.

The rationale for doing so is that the investment in the intellectual capital is a sunk cost, and it therefore does not matter what the pricing is for those rights. But of course, if we took that attitude on the pricing of all products and services, we may soon find ourselves out of business.

Now, it is true that some strategic opportunities may persuade us to price intellectual capital rights substantially below their value, intending to collect compensating value in some other way. These situations can complicate data collection for a metrics program. But they shouldn't discourage us. The metrics program should be designed to accommodate such anomalies.

The metrics that I've discussed so far can be useful at the enterprise level, at the profit-and-loss center level, at the product-line level, and at the technology bundle level. They can also be useful in drawing attention to a particular valuation expert's work or the work of a group of valuation experts. Similarly, it can be used to draw attention to a program manager's, business developer's, or product line manager's pricing work.

It's important to keep in mind that pricing decisions are often made under pressure to capture an order or orders for products and services; circumstances may lead people responsible for pricing to underprice the intellectual capital rights to increase the probability of capturing the order. Metrics can be used to provide a countervailing force, as well as to help us understand how well we are doing.

In an industry such as aerospace and defense, in which the products have historically been hardware-and-engineering-services-centric, there may be a cultural and habitual tendency to license intellectual capital for substantially less than its value. But as the business models of an industry shift, what has been a mildly bad habit can turn dangerous to the profitability and even the longevity of an enterprise.

Another important level for metrics consideration is below the profit-and-loss-center: at the level of the program office, product line, and individual. Metrics can and should be deployed to encourage program managers, business developers, and product line managers to optimize the value of the company's investments. The organization should be challenged at every level in this regard, particularly if it has a culture of providing intellectual capital rights for prices that are generally below the value of those rights.

But introducing metrics that will support the desired changes in intellectual capital management will not be the only approach beneficial to achieving successful change. There are many elements one should consider, if one wants to move an organization toward managing intellectual capital better. We consider some of these additional measures in the next chapter.

Chapter Twelve:
Change Management

Change before you have to.
> —**Jack Welch:** Source unknown

Leadership produces change. That is its primary function.
> —**John. P. Kotter:** *Force for Change: How Leadership*
> *Differs from Management* (2008)

If you want to make enemies, try to change something.
> —**Woodrow Wilson:** Source unknown

A Very Short Story: At the risk of over-informing the difficulty of change, I ask you to recall the following passage from Marcel Proust's monumental novel, *Remembrance of Things Past.* In it, the "I" of the novel recalls a recurring scene from his walks with his parents, as a child: "Presently the course of the Vivonne became choked with water-plants. At first they appeared singly, a lily, for instance, which the current, across whose path it has unfortunately grown, would never leave at rest for a moment, so that, like a ferryboat mechanically propelled, it would drift over to one bank only to return to the other, eternally repeating its double journey. Thrust towards the bank, its stalk would be straightened out, lengthened, strained almost to the breaking-point until the current again caught it, its green moorings swung back over their anchorage and brought the unhappy plant to what might fitly be called its starting-point, since it was fated not to rest there a moment before moving off once again. I would still find it there, on one walk after another, always in the same helpless state, suggesting certain victims of neurasthenia, among whom my grandfather would have included my aunt Leonie, who present without modification, year after year, the spectacle of their odd and unaccountable habits, which they always imagine themselves to be on the point of shaking off, but which they always retain to the end; caught in the treadmill of their own maladies and eccentricities, their futile endeavors to escape serve only to actuate its mechanism, to keep in motion the clockwork of their strange, ineluctable, fatal daily round. Such as these was the water-lily, and also like one of those wretches whose peculiar torments, repeated indefinitely throughout eternity, aroused the curiosity of Dante, who would have inquired of them at greater length and in fuller detail from the victims themselves, had not Virgil, striding on ahead, obliged him to hasten after him at full speed, as I must hasten after my parents."

The moral of this story? Perhaps it is this: change is hard, even—or perhaps especially—for those who would benefit most from it.

Introduction

Let me be the first to say that it is difficult to implement a comprehensive intellectual capital management system across an enterprise. Even when done in such a way as to leave profit-and-loss-center management fully in control of pricing intellectual capital rights and even when intellectual capital management policies and processes are developed with the full knowledge and representation of all stakeholder organizations and disciplines; still it is difficult.

There are three sources of this difficulty. First, any significant change is hard because it requires people to make a change in themselves, and people don't like to change. People don't like it when others—their leaders or their peers or their subordinates—tell them that they need to change. People sometimes see such a request as rude. They can see it as an attack on their autonomy, their freedom, and their competence.

Second, intellectual capital is difficult to see and think about, especially if all your senses and knowledge and understanding and intuition and education and peers and work history are attuned to a tangibles-oriented world. It can be pretty abstract stuff, difficult to think about and to converse with others about, write about, make presentations about, and sell. What people learn is easily lost, without constant reinforcement and reminders. One must, like Sisyphus, roll the huge boulder of one's ignorance up the mountain, again and again. Competent people simply do not like feeling less than fully competent. (There's a theme here, isn't there.)

Third, there is the matter of power and control. Senior business leaders don't like to be told what to do by corporate weenies. They don't like to add new metrics to the stack they are tracking. They don't like it when others make their jobs harder to do. By the way, I've seen corporate weenies banished to outer darkness by senior business leaders for daring to try to get them to change—for shining a bright light of some kind on what they are doing that is clearly less-than-optimal for the company.

So what should one do to keep from ending up under the bus or under a whole fleet of buses? What should one do if one wants to arabesque from the front end of one runaway bus to another and another and finally out of the way altogether with a fully deployed fleet of buses doing a whooshing bully blue whale of a business in intellectual capital management? Here are a few thoughts on the matter.

Making Allies of the Company's Senior Leaders

First and foremost, one must speak to a company's senior leaders from data. So, you'll need to collect data on the company's intellectual capital management slip-ups (with no attribution) or sub-optimal incidents, events, or transactions. This may be anecdotal or if you are lucky, there may be some statistical information. Best case: you may be able to collect so much anecdotal information that you can analyze it from a statistical perspective. Theoretical won't work here. You need real information about real events in the company's history that demonstrate the potential benefit of doing intellectual capital management better.

You'll need to make clear that the objective of the changes you are proposing to make to the company's policies and business processes and organization around intellectual capital management are designed, first and foremost, to inform the company's senior leaders of what is really happening to their intellectual capital so that they can make better business decisions. Your objective is to make their intellectual capital visible to them and to their employees, thereby helping them make financially better decisions about their transactions, their relationships, and the deployment of their employees' know-how.

You will want to show these senior leaders that the net effect of the changes you are proposing will make their employees better stewards of their intellectual capital—smarter and more aware and better equipped to make better decisions themselves about the management of their intellectual capital. You will want to show how their employees will be better prepared to have informed business discussions with their business partners about the intellectual capital rights that are often at the heart of the company's relationships with these business partners. You will want to show how the business policies and processes you propose will significantly reduce the possibility of rogue actors in their organizations giving away or putting at risk hundreds of millions of dollars in intellectual capital rights without the senior leaders' awareness and agreement.

You will want to make one or more of the company's senior leaders your advocate, champion, and mentor. So, focusing your campaign on this person first may make very good sense. The chief financial officer is a good candidate, perhaps the best choice in many situations. But it depends on the politics and dynamics of your particular company. Perhaps it is the chief technical officer. Or perhaps it is the senior vice president of corporate development. You could try to make all three strong supporters, but that could take a lot of consensus-building work.

Making the case for change will require data, but it also requires advocacy from others—people within the company's business units, as well as its shared services organizations. You will need to socialize your data and build advocacy broadly across the enterprise so that middle managers are also telling their senior leaders that the changes you propose would be beneficial. There are a variety of ways of doing this. One way is to develop a cross-enterprise team (or several teams) to collect relevant data through interviews or documentary research. Once you have enough data of a convincing sort, and once you have advocacy at the company's mid-levels, you can then build advocacy at the senior levels.

A change algorithm that will be important with a company's business leaders is to make clear that you will provide them with information about their transactions that they haven't had—the value of the intellectual capital rights in the transactions that are brought to them for pricing approval. The appeal is this: you will give them important information about the value of the intellectual capital rights in their transactions, which until now may have been invisible. They can then make informed decisions about pricing of those rights. Why would any senior leader say he doesn't want such relevant information?

Providing them with this information will entail developing company policy and procedures that will direct the appropriate business-people to engage the intellectual capital valuation experts in appropriate circumstances and to use the valuations provided to determine the appropriate level within the business hierarchy of the company (delegation of authority) for review and pricing of those rights. Typically, price will determine the appropriate level for decision-making on hardware and engineering services offers.

But in the area of intellectual capital, it is value, rather than price, that should determine who will need to review the proposed pricing of the intellectual capital rights, at least when providing those rights to others. (Imagine the alternative: that delegation of authority for pricing of intellectual capital rights to others should be based on price. So, if I'm a program manager and want to win a program, why wouldn't I want to price $1B of intellectual capital rights at nothing, in order to win my "must-win" order? That way, no one above me in the corporate hierarchy will review the intellectual capital rights portion of my transaction.)

Keep in mind that a company's senior leaders typically are not as bothered about territorial issues and competency insecurities as are the people working for them. They are more focused on the mission of the company itself and its economic performance than they are on these intermediate concerns. And they are good at learning new things; that's one of the skills they have had to demonstrate to become senior leaders.

What works with senior leaders—as with anyone, really—are stories, anecdotes about actual company situations involving intellectual capital management. They bring the abstract to life. Stories can help develop emotion around the quite reasonable economic arguments and risk management arguments that one routinely makes. Stories having to do with unreasonable customer or supplier demands will develop a sense of enterprise allegiance and a bias against unfair treatment. Stories having to do with theft and misuse can engender these and other "circle-the-wagons" type of emotions.

Stories involving fair and courteous behavior on the part of both licensor and licensee that end with reasonable financial benefit to both parties—happily-ever-after type stories—can lay down a path to good feeling. Such stories can affirm that good outcomes are possible through the use of best practices and an understanding of the perspectives of others. Such stories can teach that good intellectual capital management is not a pit fight but rather a matter of finding common cause.

Stories can be used to make the case that the current state of intellectual capital management isn't working very well and that with attention it can be improved. Urgency can be created by the magnitude of the potential financial benefit or loss. Stories make dollars matter emotionally, not just fiscally. Stories can help establish what doing the right thing looks like in the context of intellectual capital management and can picture the corporate hero as someone who thoughtfully and considerately looks out for the intellectual capital value of the company. By doing so, the corporate hero is really looking out for the interests of friends and colleagues in the company, family and colleagues' families, and by extension, the community of the company's business partners.

Anecdotes are important all the way through the journey, from making the initial case for change through maintenance of competence and momentum years into the change. They are important to everyone who needs to do something different and better. Human beings relate to stories and are activated by them. And we don't necessarily tire of them, as long as they are superficially novel and touch our sense of allegiance, fairness, generosity, benevolence, and achievement, or the opposite of these.

Making allies of the company's senior leaders requires both a mix of argument—evidence and logic—and anecdotes. To be your effective allies, they must be touched regularly and their allegiance thereby renewed.

One way to do this is to give them communication tasks. Perhaps you develop email content or blog content or video scripts that they can use to remind and inspire the employees who report to them about the importance of doing intellectual capital management well. Perhaps some of this content should contain pertinent questions that they expect their leaders to ask in pricing reviews. Further, they might even help their employees understand what good answers to those pertinent questions might look like.

Other content might be success stories celebrating the intellectual capital management heroes on their teams. Or perhaps they might like to relate discussions they may have had with business partners concerning intellectual capital and its value. Showing their employees how to have such conversations can be very helpful. They might also like to talk about how the business models are changing in their part of the industry and how intellectual capital management considerations are an important part of responding to these changes.

Another way to keep senior leaders engaged is with metrics. If you can get relevant intellectual capital metrics on their performance assessment dashboards, they will talk about how they are doing with their staffs. They will therefore remain engaged and attentive, as long as the metrics deliver useful and actionable information. And by focusing on relevant metrics, they will demonstrate to their staffs that good intellectual capital management is important. Their staffs can, in turn, communicate a sense of intellectual capital management's importance down through the organization.

Organizational and Personal Objectives

We have already discussed the importance of establishing organizational and personal objectives regarding intellectual capital management in the metrics section, but the subject may benefit from a little more discussion. Without objectives relating to intellectual capital management performance at an organizational and personal level, people will tend to pay less attention. But the difficulty here is that you—dear reader—are most likely not the CEO or a director of the company. You are not—most likely—in the C-suite of the company. And even if you are in the C-Suite, if you are one of the peripheral players—leaders of corporate services, rather than a profit-and-loss-center leader—you will also have significant political difficulty advancing this line of thinking. So as a practical matter, in most roles in your company, you will have a heck of a time attempting to establish organizational and personal objectives around intellectual capital management.

God speed. I wish you well in your attempts to make this happen. Success here certainly is possible over time. And the approach has a higher probability of being taken up, if the CEO and the senior profit-and-loss-center leaders come up with the idea themselves. But there are some strategies that are potentially more firmly in your grasp—that can be prosecuted early in the change process—and that can be surprisingly successful. We discuss them below.

Awards

Inventors are routinely provided awards from the company; why not intellectual capital management heroes? I'm thinking here of people who have gone out of their way and have made a significant contribution, either on the transaction side or on the relationship management side. People who make an extra effort to protect company intellectual capital, extract reasonable value from intellectual capital, or spend less than the calculated value for intellectual capital rights should be candidates for such awards. The financial awards should be comparable to the awards the company makes to inventors for their invention disclosures, patent applications, and patent awards. Managers should make a big deal about such awards, perhaps making these awards at staff meetings, bringing positive attention to the intellectual capital hero.

Overcoming Organizational Behavior

However your company is structured, the change needs to be perceived as originating from inside one's home organization, whether that is a profit-and-loss center or corporate function or shared service. Enrolling senior leaders in the change management project from all such organizational units is important for this reason. The leaders of an organizational unit can't afford for their employees to get the impression that they are simply following corporate direction. Rather, they must consistently show their teams how doing intellectual capital management well benefits them and their organization.

It's usual for organizations to develop hostility toward other organizations when a change is called for externally. Organizations and individuals are prone to suspicion and negativity when a change is perceived to be imposed. To counteract this, the leadership of each group of workers needs to cultivate advocacy, to be perceived as an advocate. Each leader must own the change and must believe that becoming better at intellectual capital management is the right thing to do.

Boundaries and Control

In other words, each organization or group within an organization must understand that it is fundamentally in control of its own priorities and its own integrity. Within the context of its becoming a better intellectual capital management organization, it should perceive that it is captain of its own ship. The pace of change, the nature of the change priorities that it endeavors to take on and implement, the depth of its thinking about its intellectual capital management issues, and the implications for how it does its business should be in its own control. Yes, it should report on relevant metrics, and its reporting is certainly where control meets accountability. Reporting is where an organization's commitment to the change becomes visible to others, where its own seriousness can be observed. Visibility is a good thing in the dark and murky world of intangibles. Anything one can do to increase visibility is positive. Metrics can help in this regard.

Audit

To make big changes in an organization—the sort of changes we're talking about here, at least in some companies—one (everyone) must be able clearly to answer the following question: "what's in it for me?" (WIIFM). Awards and praise can help with this. So can metrics. So can leadership's regular endorsement and reinforcement of the change. And so can maintaining an organization's boundaries and its sense of self-control, thereby reinforcing its integrity. But there's nothing like regular audits to focus the mind.

If there is one thing people do not like, it's being singled out for a deficiency on an internal audit report that is widely distributed. When this happens, it's like someone just got a bad grade, and almost everyone who matters in a person's annual performance assessment is made aware of it. Not good. In fact people will go to great lengths to avoid this circumstance. If audits in the field of intellectual capital management are used regularly, you would be surprised how fast the organization changes. The WIIFM question is answered definitively using this approach.

So in lieu of establishing organizational and personal objectives, establishing regular audits concerning the enterprise's performance according to its intellectual capital management policies and business processes can be very effective.

Conclusion

When it happens, organizational change is always motivated by someone somewhere within the company. Where best to locate the intellectual capital management advocates and experts? How best to think about their organizational role? What authority and responsibility should they have? How should we position them for success in the change management journey we are asking the company to take? We have touched on some of these questions already, but a couple remain. We address them briefly in the next chapter.

Chapter Thirteen:
Organization

Every company has two organizational structures: The formal one is written on the charts; the other is the everyday relationship of the men and women in the organization.

—Harold S. Geneen: *Managing* (1985)

Reorganization to me is shuffling boxes around. Transformation means that you're really fundamentally changing the way the organization thinks, the way it responds, the way it leads. It's a lot more than just playing with the boxes.

—Louis V. Gerstner: "In Focus: Lou Gerstner"
—An interview with Richard Quest on CNN (July 2, 2004)

A Very Short Story: As I have thought about company organization structure over the years—regarding the place of intellectual capital management in it—an analogy emerged between this question and the question of how to organize a piece of writing—its organizational design, if you will, and the concision and clarity with which it is executed. (Perhaps I go a little far afield sometimes to reason by analogy. But when one goes far afield, what one occasionally finds can be worth the trek.) Then I began to think about Strunk and White's *Elements of Style,* which was first self-published by William Strunk Jr. when he was a professor more than 100 years ago at Cornell University. E.B. White edited it and significantly expanded it in the late 1950s. Macmillan published the first edition of this new, collaborative version in 1959. In one of my college writing classes, I too was taught from a then-current edition of this little book. A couple of passages from that book may make sense to repeat here. The first is this: "A sonnet is built on a fourteen-line frame, each line containing five feet. Hence, the sonneteer knows exactly where he is headed, although he may not know how to get there. Most forms of composition are less clearly defined, more flexible, but all have skeletons to which the writer will bring the flesh and blood. The more clearly he perceives the shape, the better are his chances of success." Here is the second: "Vigorous writing is concise. A sentence should contain no unnecessary words, a paragraph no unnecessary sentences, for the same reason that a drawing should have no unnecessary lines and a machine no unnecessary parts. This requires not that the writer make all his sentences short, or that he avoid all detail and treat his subjects only in outline, but that every word tell."

The moral of this story? Perhaps it is this: words and other symbols are the world for us. They are largely how we experience, understand, and structure the world so that it is malleable—so that it is manageable. The design of the firm's organization—what the parts are and how they relate to one another—is therefore not terribly unlike the structure of a sonnet or a business process description or an essay on the theory of the firm. The organization chart itself is a verbal and graphical structure telling the members of the firm how they are to work together and how the work is to be divided up to accomplish the objectives of the enterprise.

Introduction

Where to put the intellectual capital management people? First, their function is a business rather than legal or contracts function, as I suggested in Chapter Four. Second, they perform a role that is, in the main, consultative rather than operational. But a caveat is warranted here: a group of intellectual capital management people could function as deal-makers for a variety of intellectual-capital-centric cross-enterprise relationship types. Examples might be joint ventures, strategic alliances, joint developments, product line divestitures or purchases, and out-of-market licensing.

Think of the intellectual capital management group a bit like your mergers and acquisitions (M&A) group, except they specialize in intellectual-capital-intensive transactions that do not involve the purchase or sale of equity assets. The assets in which they specialize are intellectual capital rights.

Intellectual-capital-intensive transactions can be very different from equity-based transactions. For example, a senior financial leader (who had been involved in compliance and M&A work) in one of the companies I have worked for was astonished that I could negotiate a licensing transaction involving immature technology (technology that had not been fully productized) and that could easily turn out to be material to his business unit. He accorded almost no value to the subject intellectual capital rights until I successfully negotiated the terms of the transaction. Then when I showed him the financial analysis (including a reasonable discount rate, given the risks) based on the value of the intellectual capital assets, and walked him through it, he was flabbergasted.

What is reasonable to expect from intellectual-capital-intensive transactions is not at all clear to people whose deal-making experience and expertise is outside of this field.

So, depending on the strategic importance of particular joint ventures, strategic alliances, and joint developments, it may make sense to consider selecting the deal-maker for such transactions from the cadre of intellectual capital management experts. In large companies, it may make sense to consider asking such people to lead cross-enterprise deals of these kinds (deals in which the intellectual capital involved may come from or could have significant effects on multiple profit and loss centers).

To my second point above—that the intellectual capital management people will provide a consultative rather than operational function—I'm getting at the idea that a key role for this group is facilitating, mentoring, educating, and coaching. In other words, because there is virtually no education in the field of intellectual capital management in our universities, such education needs to be provided by a cadre of experts on-the-job.

Yes, a series of courses can be developed and taught in-house or obtained from such professional organizations as the Licensing Executives Society, USA and Canada (LES), but courses aren't enough to develop the working experience and expertise that many intellectual-capital-centric enterprises need. Adults do have a difficult time with rigorous academic courses and seem to learn much more effectively through an on-the-job and just-in-time education approach—a learn-by-doing sort of method.

And this is where the cadre of intellectual capital management experts comes in. These professionals can provide coaching and facilitation services and even project management services under the authority of a business unit leader or leaders. By operating in this way, these experts can—over time—transfer much of their intellectual capital management expertise to the organization's operational business leaders.

Third, the intellectual capital management group could also lead the development of business policies and processes needed to promote the efficient and effective management of intellectual capital across the enterprise.

Fourth, the intellectual capital management group could lead the development of education and communication concerned with excellence in intellectual capital management, targeting many levels within the organization: from senior leaders down to individual contributors.

So, as I say, where to put them?

Legal

Because intellectual capital management is a business rather than a legal function, putting such a group in the legal department, under the authority of lawyers, may not be the best choice. Lawyers are educated to focus on minimization of risk and on strong—some may say extreme—client advocacy. The role of intellectual capital management—when the function is deployed in a deal-making or deal-consulting role—is actually to find a middle ground, where the needs of both parties are met. The deal-maker's role is to make the deal happen, if it is worth doing, rather than to identify all the terms that are unacceptable to the enterprise. The role of the intellectual capital management team is to teach operational business leaders how to negotiate sometimes complicated intellectual-capital-intensive relationships in such a way that each of the parties understands the perspective of the other(s) and respects that perspective.

Often, a deal will not be a one-and-done affair. It will be one of many deals one can anticipate making over a period of years or decades with the same party or parties. Negotiating a deal in this context means allowing the parties to come away with a sense that they were treated fairly. One can be a sharp negotiator without inspiring a residual hostility. Management of the relationship for the long term is paramount.

In my experience in several companies, the legal department will sometimes take an extreme position, which can be deleterious to a longer-term relationship. The negotiating style that I've sometimes seen from lawyers is brusque and adversarial, rather than collaborative. Again, in the context of developing and reinforcing a durable relationship, an adversarial style can work against the long-term objective.

In addition, lawyers are often not fundamentally quantitative (in their role as lawyers). And this makes it difficult for them to achieve a balanced perspective—balancing risk and financial benefit—in their deal-making. Their perspective often needs to be balanced by an experienced, independent, intellectual capital management person.

Finance

While the finance people are certainly quantitative, they typically play a fiscally conservative or back-office role in the enterprise, rather than a catalytic or deal-making role. While some of the work-streams of the intellectual capital management group should be designed to conserve the value of the enterprise's intellectual capital rights, the primary orientation of the group should be toward value-extraction, whether that means a focus on deal-making or business model innovation or profit enhancement through proper valuation and pricing of intangible assets and software-and-information-based products and services.

The role of the intellectual capital management group is often to improve how the enterprise thinks about and behaves toward its most valuable asset class: intellectual capital. To play this role successfully, the intellectual capital experts need to be managed by people who are attuned to the marketplace trends (whether technology-based, business-model-based, product/service-centric, value-chain-based, etc.) and are responsible for leading change in the organization to respond to those trends.

Corporate Development & Strategy

Perhaps the best organizational box or set of boxes in which to put the intellectual capital management team is in corporate development or strategy. Typically, the corporate development function includes M&A; so, it is usually deal-making in its orientation. Sometimes the corporate development group also contains a strategy development and coordination function; so much the better, since intellectual capital management work-streams tend to interact with and support strategic functions, whether at the corporate level or at the profit-and-loss-center level.

If the enterprise is large enough, there may be both a corporate-level intellectual capital management group and similar groups at the business unit level. While the corporate group might maintain a role in the cross-enterprise intellectual capital management policy and business process areas and the education, communication, and cross-enterprise deal-making and advising areas, the groups of intellectual capital management experts at the business unit level may focus on the facilitation, mentoring, educating, deal-making, and consulting areas for their specific business units.

Again, if the enterprise is large enough, there may be a public policy role for the corporate group and possibly for the business unit level groups as well. The extent of the group's involvement in public policy matters will depend on how important various areas of intellectual capital management are to the enterprise's business success—at the legislative, regulatory, and judicial levels. Sometimes, the lawyers will lead this work, and this may make perfectly good sense, but when matters of financial impact and intellectual capital value are at the heart of the matter, it will probably make sense to have the intellectual capital management experts involved. Public policy work really relates to corporate strategy; so, an important question here is where the company prefers to locate its strategy concerning the management of its intellectual capital.

Both Centralized and Distributed Control

We have mentioned the importance of power and control as a motive force in companies. In the case of intellectual capital management, we need to consider both a centralized function—let's say in the corporate development organization—and a distributed function, let's say in each of the strategic business units' strategy functions. In this approach, each of the business units has some control over its own intellectual capital management. This would be similar to the way strategic business units have responsibility over their own finance and accounting matters, while being guided by the corporate finance group. Organizing the intellectual capital management work in this way should provide both the business units and the corporate offices sufficient buy-in and control.

Beyond the Box

As we've already discussed, the intellectual capital management team will be working to change the way the enterprise thinks about and manages its most valuable asset class. This entails enlisting change agents throughout the company in an informal network of believers and proselytizers. Leaders need to support the work, but so do energized people throughout the organization. While the box in which the intellectual capital management team is placed is important, even more so are the relationships that these experts build with their business unit and shared service customers such as the program managers, product line managers, business developers, account managers, and others.

But after all, what should the priorities of the intellectual capital management team be? Once located organizationally, how should they proceed? How should they organize their thinking? A bit of this is touched on in the next chapter.

Chapter Fourteen:
In A Nutshell

I fear this little episode does not speak very favourably for my business capacity in those early days, for I certainly ought to have made much more than I did by this really important invention.
— **Henry Bessemer:** Source unknown

Invention is not enough. Tesla invented the electric power we use, but he struggled to get it out to people. You have to combine both things: invention and innovation focus, plus the company that can commercialize things and get them to people.
— **Larry Page:** An interview with Charlie Rose in *TEDBlog* (March 19, 2014)

If we could create invention capitalism, that would be a helluva legacy, that would be a helluva thing to do....We could actually turbocharge the rate at which the world invents things.
— **Nathan Myrvold:** An interview with Joe Hagan in *Men's Journal* (2012)

There is no particular scheme or framework of intellectual capital management that is the right or best scheme or framework, as far as I know. There are proposed schemes and frameworks, but that isn't what we have been about here. No, what we have been exploring is the need for a somewhat different concept of the firm and some ideas for reconfiguring or reorienting it.

Some companies are focused on intellectual capital management because they have begun with the notion that intellectual capital management is one of the core disciplines they need to be successful. Such companies may not have the phrase "intellectual capital management" in their vocabularies. That's okay, because from the beginning they have taken excellence in intellectual capital management seriously. They have built goals and processes and culture around this vital activity and sensibility.

But those companies that currently don't have a systemic focus on intellectual capital management are vulnerable. They are vulnerable to innovative competitors who do have such a focus, and they are vulnerable to the intellectual capital thieves of the world. This little book is written for people in these companies who sense that vulnerability and want to do something about it.

Such people need an explicit vocabulary to help make intellectual capital visible to the company. To move a company to an intellectual capital management orientation requires a case for change. It entails convincing people to think about things differently and to do things differently. And to do this, one can benefit from the use of some of the vocabulary I have used here.

As I have suggested, the paths and areas of early focus for such people can be quite various. The important thing, though, is to find the low hanging fruit—to find an area or areas of work for which there will be immediate perceived benefit. Early success in organizational change is important.

In some companies, the low-hanging fruit might be in collaboration and consortium relationships. In another, it might be in patent licensing. In another, it could be in developing and implementing business policies and processes concerning management of the company's intellectual capital in its commercial endeavors in China. In still another, it might consist in developing a new business model and the processes involved in delivering products or services through that new business model to the market. In another, it might mean the development of metrics to assess the velocity and quality of the company's innovation pipeline. And in still another, it might be the development of effective systematic approaches to valuing licensed products and services, such as software, information, and access.

At the heart of all this work is the sense of the value of a company's intellectual capital expressed in quantitative terms. Doing the work entails a sense of urgency—a bias for meaningful and effective action. In prosecuting this work, one should demand expediency over bureaucracy, speed over tediousness. One must find short-cuts and rules of thumb timely to meet the pace of business decision-making that is driven by one's competitors and customers. One must not delay the organization but rather keep pace with its drive toward continued success.

Intellectual capital management, when done well, is practical more than philosophical, although it is based on the philosophical notion that a company's real value is in its intellectual capital and the methods by which the enterprise chooses to innovate, expand, protect, and deploy that capital. When a cadre of intellectual capital management experts is delivering real value to the company, this group will be hard-nosed, hard-driving, focused, patient, persistent, generous, kind, incisive, innovative, collaborative, and relentless. Above all this group will be smart and will exhibit unusual organizational courage. It will be politically astute, driving toward developing the critical information the company's leadership needs to make the best decisions for the company, and at the same time helping the company plug the holes to prevent unnecessary intellectual capital leakage.

The cadre of intellectual capital management experts will be a group of entrepreneurs focused on helping the company to innovate its bundle of intellectual capital and to preserve, enhance, and capture the value of that intellectual capital better over time. I like a quote from Peter Drucker here, taken from a paper of his published in the *Harvard Business Review* (August, 2002): "Today, much confusion exists about the proper definition of entrepreneurship. Some observers use the term to refer to all small businesses; others, to all new businesses. In practice, however, a great many well-established businesses engage in highly successful entrepreneurship. The term, then, refers not to an enterprise's size or age but to a certain kind of activity. At the heart of the activity is innovation: the effort to create purposeful, focused change in an enterprise's economic or social potential."

In the abstract, it really doesn't matter where one begins to improve a company's management of its intellectual capital. It's the actual beginning that's important. As one hammers away with one's beak on the roof of the enterprise, one will learn what one needs to know.

But the school of hard knocks is not sufficient preparation to do the work I propose. A good deal of reading and learning is also required, because others have done a great deal of relevant thinking and study that can give us a powerful head-start (so to speak). To this end, a suggested reading list is provided in the next section.

Chapter Fifteen:
Suggested Reading

I have always imagined that paradise will be a kind of library.
—**Jorge Luis Borges:** Source unknown

If you are going to get anywhere in life, you have to read a lot of books.
—**Roald Dahl:** Source unknown

I find television very educating. Every time someone turns on the set, I go into the other room and read a book.
—**Groucho Marx:** Source unknown

There is much to read in the field of intellectual capital management. There are two periodicals of particular note for business people:
- *IAM Magazine*
- *les Nouvelles*, which is published by LES International and which is only available to members of the thirty-plus LES societies around the world.

And there are many books that provide important information and insightful perspectives. I recommend the following, in roughly the order presented below:
- *Valuation and Dealmaking of Technology-Based Intellectual Property: Principals, Methods, and Tools,* Richard Razgaitis, Wiley, Second Edition (2009).
- *Intellectual Property: Valuation, Exploitation, and Infringement Damages, 2016 Cumulative Supplement,* Russell Parr, Wiley, Twelfth Edition (2016).
- *BVR's Guide to Intellectual Property Valuation, Second Edition,* Michael Pellegrino, Business Valuation Resources, Second Edition (2012).
- *Patent Valuation: Improving Decision Making through Analysis,* William J. Murphy, John L. Orcutt, and Paul C. Remus, Wiley Finance (2012).
- *Intangible Capital: Putting Knowledge to Work in the 21st-Century Organization,* Mary Adams & Michael Oleksak, Praeger (2010).

- *Value-Driven Intellectual Capital: How to Convert Intangible Corporate Assets into Market Value,* Patrick H. Sullivan, Wiley (2000).
- *Managing Intellectual Capital: Organizational, Strategic, and Policy Dimensions (Clarendon Lectures in Management Studies),* David J. Teece, Oxford University Press (2001).
- *Capitalism Without Capital: The Rise of the Intangible Economy,* Jonathan Haskel and Stian Westlake, Princeton University Press (2017).
- *The End of Accounting and the Path Forward for Investors and Managers,* Baruch Lev and Feng Gu, Wiley (2016).
- *A Triumph of Genius: Edwin Land, Polaroid, and the Kodak Patent War,* Ronald K. Fierstein, Ankerwycke (2015).
- *The Invisible Edge: Taking Your Strategy to the Next Level Using Intellectual Property,* Mark Blaxill and Ralph Eckardt, Portfolio Hardcover (2009).
- *Edison in the Boardroom Revisited: How Leading Companies Realize Value from their Intellectual Property,* Susan S. Harrison and Patrick H. Sullivan, Wiley (2011).
- *The Qualcomm Equation: How a Fledgling Telecom Company Forged a New Path to Big Profits and Market,* Dave Mock, AMACOM (2005).
- *Burning the Ships: Intellectual Property and the Transformation of Microsoft,* Marshall Phelps and David Kline, Wiley (2009).
- *Negotiating the Impossible: How to Break Deadlocks and Resolve Ugly Conflicts (Without Money or Muscle),* Deepak Malhotra, Berrett-Koehler (2016).
- *The Innovator's Dilemma: When New Technologies Cause Great Firms to Fail,* Clayton M. Christensen, Harvard Business Review Press (2013).
- *How Innovation Really Works: Using the Trillion-Dollar R&D Fix to Drive Growth,* Anne Marie Knott, McGraw Hill Education (2016).
- *Reinvent Your Business Model: How to Seize the White Space for Transformative Growth,* Mark W. Johnson, Harvard Business Review Press (2018).
- *The Heart of Change: Real-Life Stories of How People Change Their Organizations,* John P. Kotter and Dan S. Cohen, Harvard Business Review Press (2012).
- *The Advantage: Why Organizational Health Trumps Everything Else in Business,* Patrick Lencioni, Jossey-Bass (2012).
- *Secrets: Managing Information Assets in the Age of Cyberespionage,* James Pooley, Verus Press (2015).
- *Patent Law Essentials: A Concise Guide,* Alan L. Durham, Praeger, Fifth Edition (2018).
- *Emanuel Law Outlines: Intellectual Property,* Margreth Barrett, Aspen Publishers, Third Edition (2012).

I order them this way because one does want to read the most important material first, and one wants the early material to provide a foundation for what one will learn later. So, the quantitative work comes first, and the legal perspective comes last.

This is fitting, since we are talking about a business function, when we talk about intellectual capital management.

I recommend you read these books critically but with enthusiasm. Each contains many pearls of great value.

Again, we are preparing business people to do the work of intellectual capital management. To do this work, you will need to know something about the legal protections, but you should also have contracts, subcontracts, and legal specialists to rely on. So, we are light on the legal matters.

The field of quality management and business process design and improvement is not addressed in the list above, but the serious student of intellectual capital management should read in this important area. There are a variety of quality management and business process design and development disciplines, such as Total Quality Management, Lean Electronics, Six Sigma, and Quality Function Deployment. The serious student should become expert at the use of one or more of these or a like methodology (each with its own toolset). So also should the serious student read up on voluntary consensus standards and the ANSI Essential Requirements, since the development and use of such standards in intellectual capital management will likely become a significant aspect of the field.

An additional area not mentioned in the list above that should also be considered is the licensing of intellectual capital. There are many useful books in this area that cover different kinds of licenses, different terms and conditions, the use of term sheets, and so forth. But keep in mind that as the business expert in intellectual capital management, you should not try to become expert in licensing terms. You really should look to the lawyers and contracts folks for an expert-level understanding in this important area.

Further, my assumption is that you know your way around a spreadsheet and a net present value analysis, that you have done reading in the field of business strategy, and that you have some understanding of an enterprise balance sheet and income statement. In other words, I'm assuming that you have either gone through an MBA program or that you have done the reading to give you the basic business education you will need to do well in intellectual capital management.

Some of the books above may be difficult to get, while others are merely expensive. So be it.

In any case, the knowledge provided by them will give you valuable insights in how to deliver superior value to your enterprise. And they will help give a shape to your thinking about the field of intellectual capital management.

Are there other books in the field that you should consider reading? Certainly. There are additional existing books that you should consider, and as the field advances, there will be others. The list above is simply a reasonably good place to start.

One final area of importance: the Licensing Executives Society, USA and Canada, web site. With a membership in this professional organization, you will have access to many publications, webinars, courses, conferences, and documentary resources that will be of benefit. The members are overwhelmingly friendly and helpful, anxious to support others in their learning and their work in the field of intellectual capital management. Here is the website: https://www.lesusacanada.org/

Afterword

Some Personal Endnotes

After reading an earlier version of this book in manuscript form, a friend asked me to clarify my background, because it wasn't clear from what weird avian or reptilian perspective I might be offering my suggestions in this compendium. So at the risk of droning on and on about what is to me (and probably to you) a very dull subject, let me give you the following information.

I've worked in three Fortune 500 companies and a startup. All of the three larger companies have been, as I say, in the field of aerospace and defense. I've worked in two electronics systems R&D labs—one hardware and the other software—a variety of profit-and-loss centers, and in a centralized corporate function—a corporate development organization that reported directly to the CEO. There, I reported to the head of corporate development. The lead people for mergers and acquisitions, strategy, and corporate communications were all my peers.

Throughout my career, my responsibilities have been fairly diverse: engineering management, procurement, business development/marketing, program management, product line management, licensing (both out and in), strategic planning, operations planning, and intellectual capital management.

Early in my career, I worked closely with patent attorneys to secure patent rights for inventions we developed leading up to proposal submission to commercial companies and US government agencies to secure technology development contracts. In those R&D labs, I was essentially the patent committee lead, along with the patent attorney. We not only filed applications for patents on soon-to-be-revealed inventions in bid situations but also inventions made in the more standard, run-of-the-mill R&D programs.

In the first of these labs—the hardware lab—I had the good fortune to work with a very smart, humble, good-humored, and generous patent attorney. Over an apprenticeship of five or six years, he showed me the ropes and steered me in my reading, tutoring me in intellectual property matters, helping me to understand the nature of the concerns and competencies a business person should have to manage the company's intellectual property well. He taught me the difference between intellectual property and other corporate intellectual capital, and he taught me how to approach all forms of intellectual capital.

Following my intellectual property and intellectual capital management education from my lawyer friend, I became involved with negotiating intellectual capital rights with customers and co-development partners. I functioned then, sometimes, as a consultant to bid teams, helping to coach others in discussion and negotiation concerning intellectual capital rights. I also was involved with bid strategy and proposal strategy concerning these efforts to secure technology development contracts.

As the business development person on a few of these pursuits, I had lead responsibility, along with the program managers involved, in negotiating these rights, in addition to pricing matters for intellectual capital rights and engineering services and work scope.

I've also spent a good deal of time in licensing purgatory. I'm not sure whether you are familiar with *Rembrandts in the Attic: Unlocking the Hidden Value of Patents*. The authors are Kevin Rivette and David Kline. The book was published in 1999. This put many of us in the field of intellectual capital management in licensing purgatory for years, maybe decades in some cases. There were preceding business publications that popularized the patent licensing work being done at RCA and Texas Instruments, where hundreds of millions of dollars or more were annually being generated from patent and other forms of licensing.

The concept here was to go searching around in the intellectual property attic and bring downstairs all the paintings that were hidden up there and that could be used to drop huge quantities of cash into the company's income statement. Magic money from the magic intellectual property place, in the eyes of company CEOs.

This has been characterized as "the crack cocaine" of intellectual capital management. CEOs love this sort of thing, because apparently (according to the early stories) for very little in incremental investment, they thought they would get a lot of "free" money to drop to the bottom line. A few companies received a lot of press on this approach. And a few operating companies continue to use patent licensing as a significant augmentation to their primary business models.

But most operating companies can't make this model work on an ongoing basis. There isn't sufficient market share or investment or human capital or management commitment or tolerance for litigation risk or tolerance for business partner risk or innovation or more likely a combination of these to make this revenue and profit generation approach work on a sustainable basis. In other words, most companies do not have a sufficient number of Rembrandts painting up there in their attics to keep up an art factory that would sustain an ongoing business model in patent and other forms of technology licensing that would have a material effect on the company's financials. Most companies find it sufficiently challenging to offer competitive and sufficiently profitable products and services on a sustainable basis. Besides, most senior operating company business leaders don't like to license their competitors to practice their intellectual capital against them.

Then there is the unwillingness of business leaders to relinquish control of their technology to some corporate weenie or weenies, with unforeseen consequences to their business.

So, what you see in many companies is a boom and bust cycle in the effort to generate a sustainable flow of this artistic crack cocaine revenue. People come and go. The concept comes and goes. People fail to fulfill their promises because of insufficient investment, insufficient human capital, insufficient sustained innovation, insufficient will to sue competitors, suppliers, and customers, insufficient management tolerance for litigation risk, etc. Or there is organizational conflict between the licensing people and the business unit leaders. Then the licensing people are let go.

Meanwhile, some of these companies are paying less-than-optimal attention to their strategic intellectual capital management issues. They're devoting insufficient expertise to managing their most precious source of revenue and profits: intellectual capital. They're focusing people who are knowledgeable about intellectual capital issues on tactical revenue matters—hauling down the paintings and selling them—rather than on helping the company to adjust its business policies, processes, business models, strategy, tools, education, and norms to accommodate an intellectual-capital-centric future.

During my career, I was caught up in this a couple of times, in a couple of different companies over a period of decades, starting back in the very early 1990s. To me, for most companies, this sort of work is a colossal waste of time. In most companies, the effect on reported earnings is minimal.

I remember a conversation with one of my leaders when I made the estimate that I could perhaps generate about $10M per year in sustained licensing and patent sales revenues, if I couldn't take people to court and if I could not license our competitors. My leader's reply was right on the money, so to speak: that would be immaterial to the company. So, why bother? After that conversation, I no longer bothered. I shifted my focus exclusively to strategic management of intellectual capital and formulated an approach to what such a program should look like. But of course, this took time. This took many years of trial and error. As I say, I learned a lot more about how not to do intellectual capital management than I did about how to do it well.

And of course, the dollars associated with managing intellectual capital well vastly overwhelm the possible dollars that one can generate from artistic-crack-cocaine-type licensing. After all, we're talking about intellectual capital that represents 60-90 percent of the company's future cash flows.

So, where was I? I was talking about my experience in the field of intellectual capital management. So, I worked in a couple of labs. Worked in business development and program management and intellectual capital management. Then for a short time, I did some business development and pricing in an education business focused on software design and development. Then I blasted off for an opportunity in the attic-ascending-descending realm.

Then this morphed into a strategic planning and operations planning job for an aerospace and defense profit-and-loss center. Then more business development and program management, negotiating intellectual capital rights with business partners and customers.

Then there was a stint in a startup, where I was responsible for managing the patenting process, procurement, and program management. Then I led advanced engineering, where my team did wireless network testing and design work, giving feedback to the rest of the engineering team. (By the way, the most political work experience I ever had was in this startup.)

Then I became a corporate weenie at another large company, where once again I was expected to mount the stairs into the attic to see what I could find, along with holding the patent budget and chairing the company's patent committee. And sure, there was a lot there. But do you know what happens when the ground rules are that you will not get your company involved in litigation, and you are expected to license the company's patents? Do you know what happens when you attempt to license proprietary information and know-how to engineering companies with real-life, proud, prickly, bright engineers with a "not-invented-here" attitude? You end up trying to do technology licensing on your knees. Try that, if you haven't already. It's an educational experience, and I can personally attest that it builds character. Or rather, I can't testify to that. But my wife can. However, I'm not sure she likes the character that that experience built.

As a corporate weenie, I began to put into play a bunch of the stuff I'd learned in my earlier gigs, pertaining to the more strategic concept of intellectual capital management. As I say, for many years, I was chair of the company's patent committee. I led a cross-enterprise team to put together a business process for management of third-party software and a business process for management of open source software. Then I hired several very bright, energetic people. We benchmarked at a number of companies, including Philips, AT&T, Microsoft, and others. We read a lot of excellent books. We put together a program focused on how to do intellectual capital management in a strategic way, rather than a mounting-the-stairs-to-the-attic way and a crawling-around-on-one's-knees way.

We collected stories from around the company on situations that were sub-optimal: transactions and escapes, primarily. We put together cross-enterprise teams to do this. We collected information on who was doing what and on what had gone well and not so well in intellectual capital transactions. We communicated with senior company leaders directly. We built a constituency among middle management folks who were part of the fact-finding teams. We built the case that the company could do the management of its intellectual capital better in transactions and on-going work with its business partners. We demonstrated that people often did not have a handle on the value of intellectual capital rights when discussing and negotiating such rights. Sometimes no one really had responsibility for the financial end of all this—for making sure the company either paid or was paid a reasonable value for the rights in question.

As our role evolved, it turned out that there were business processes that had not really been optimized, regarding the management of the company's intellectual capital. We discovered this, in particular, in the context of our joint ventures, but we found that this was also true of quotidian relationships with customers, suppliers, government agencies, and others. Often the business policies and processes in place could be improved. So, we worked on that with the various stakeholders in those processes.

As we pressed into all this, we found that there were no standards to guide our procurement people or contracts people or lawyers or business-people, when it came to custodianship of others' intellectual capital and others' custodianship of our intellectual capital. There were no standards concerning what was acceptable from a business policy and process perspective in the management of others' proprietary information. So, we dug into that.

We discovered similar things about the valuation and pricing approval of intellectual capital rights. So, we dug into that as well. We dug into that in both the technology domain and in the intangible products and services domain (e.g., software, software as a service, information and data as a service, and network access as a service).

We actually began all of this in the aftermarket, developing improved approaches to understanding the value of the various intellectual capital rights transactions the company had been doing there, aiming to provide senior leaders with financial insight into the consequences of these transactions. With that improved insight, the notion was that they would be able to make pricing decisions with a clearer idea of the financial reasonableness and business impact.

There's a lot more that one could go into, but maybe that's enough for now.

Along the way, what we found was that the lawyers are not enough. That there need to be business/financial experts working on this sort of thing. What we found was that the lawyers will sometimes focus on the legal issues and miss the business and financial and practical, nuts-and-bolts issues. What we found was that comprehensive business policy and process around the management of the company's critical intellectual capital could be improved. Finally, we found that even coming to an understanding of what is critical and non-critical in the company's intellectual capital store simply wasn't happening in an optimal way.

We learned that in an effort to make business partners happy, some business and technical people provided significantly greater intellectual capital rights than their leaders were aware. Or they paid more for intellectual rights than they needed to. Or they priced intellectual capital rights being made available to others lower than the actual value. And, again, we found that a quantitative valuation assessment could often be helpful to everyone involved in thinking through the strategy for such business partner interactions.

(Is any of this unusual? No. Not in the least. It's quite usual at the companies for which I've worked, in the industry in which I've worked, and in many other industries, as far as I can tell. In other words, there is no news here. Not in my experience. Many companies can do better in these areas and can benefit significantly from doing so.)

So, we mounted a program to do better in these areas.

What was my office's role? Well mostly it was consultative. Mostly it was to develop business policy, process, tools, education, communication, and mentoring in these and other areas. Sometimes it was to lead out-licensing transactions. But this was very rare. We consulted on both out-licensing and in-licensing transactions, as well as joint development/joint ownership situations. Our way into the discussion was often the requirement for a valuation of the intellectual capital rights that needed to be presented to senior leadership and approved at a pricing meeting.

We also developed a public policy role, over time. The strategy here was to influence the industry and to influence Congress and the regulators. We did that through involvement with a trade association (the Intellectual Property Committee of the Aerospace Industries Association) and with LES, in our support of LES Standards. Our theory was that the development and application of standards in the management of intellectual capital would improve things for everyone. A rising tide lifts all boats, type of deal.

Lessons Learned

What have I learned from all this? Well, first, it's this: in some (maybe many) companies, there's a significant strategic opportunity for value creation, capture, preservation, and risk reduction through business and financial expertise in intellectual capital management.

Second: in many companies, if you can stay out of the business of selling pictures from the company's attic, do. You and your company are likely to be much better for it.

Third: position the intellectual capital management function where it can have meaningful scope—in a corporate organization, with a reporting relationship as close to the CEO as possible. Get him or her on your side. Make sure you have the CEO's understanding and advocacy for what you are doing.

Fourth: do not challenge the profit-and-loss center leaders or the shared service organization leaders for control of their intellectual capital, for the pricing of its rights or their business partners' intellectual capital rights, or for any management responsibility for their businesses. Otherwise, you are doomed to failure, either immediately or over time, since profit-and-loss center leaders will view you as a competitor.

Fifth: the corollary to the fourth lesson is that your function must be consultative, not operational. Your office must be relied on to speak objectively about the value of the intellectual capital rights at hand and about the transactions and business processes at issue. Senior leaders must be able to rely on you to provide evidence-based insight and guidance based on the literature and best practices in the profession of intellectual capital management. You should not have profit-and-loss responsibility.

Sixth: to ensure that the business units have integrity and that they actively participate in and endorse the utility of the work, educate them and delegate to them as much of the work as possible, monitoring them periodically and supporting them when asked.

Seventh: Engage in public policy work to ensure that what you are learning gets embedded in appropriate intellectual capital management standards and cross-industry practices. Coordinate this work with your business units and shared services. Make sure they understand in what ways you are working with their business partners in standards-setting organizations, trade associations, and professional associations to make their industry and their profit and loss center better.

Eighth: the business units and shared services are your customers. Treat them that way.

Ninth: clearly define the difference between the scope of work of the intellectual capital management organization and the legal department, the contracts and subcontracts organizations, the mergers and acquisition team, and corporate finance so that there is as little unnecessary conflict as possible.

Tenth: ensure that the company policy and process concerning pricing of intellectual capital rights is developed with input from all key constituencies, that it is well understood, and that it is taught and communicated and reinforced often.

Eleventh: look for opportunities to lionize people in the business units and shared services for their work in intellectual capital management. Make heroes of those who have done well in this fire swamp.

Twelfth: keep your leadership aligned. Make sure your leadership understands the big deals and big initiatives you are supporting and leading and the risks and opportunities involved. Make sure your leadership is part of your decision-making process. Much can go wrong with the organization's understanding of intellectual capital management issues. This is not a field many people understand. Much can be misconstrued and miscommunicated. Much can go haywire. So, keep your leadership close, and don't hesitate to seek help and support when appropriate.

Thirteenth: develop allies at all levels throughout the organization and actively work to maintain these alliances. You'll need them.

Fourteenth: read and study and network like your career depends upon it, because it does.

Fifteenth: build a brand for yourself, because without a brand confirmed by the wide world outside your company, you're just another pseudo-intellectual-capital-management cake eater.

Sixteenth: define your expertise as something that is unique within your company, something no other group or discipline has. Make sure you communicate the nature of this expertise frequently, throughout the company. Make everyone aware of how you can help and that it is valuable and unobtainable elsewhere within the company. Make sure your charter for this work is endorsed by the company's senior leadership. Make sure your customers understand that you are an expert in the field of intellectual capital management and that this is a *bona fide* field, not some figment of your imagination.

Seventeenth: name the field in which you are operating "intellectual capital management" rather than "intellectual property management." Otherwise, you will confuse the heck out of everyone, including the lawyers, who will want to claim that you are trying to give legal advice and should be working for them. Adopt a "blue ocean strategy" here—a strategy to find a part of the ocean to operate in that does not have a lot of blood in the water, not a lot of competition. Adopt the name "intellectual capital management" to differentiate what you are doing from what everyone else in the company is doing and to help the company understand that change is afoot, a change in a positive direction. A change that will provide the business-people with responsibility and authority over and significant new knowledge concerning their most valuable asset class: intellectual capital.

Eighteenth: ensure that your company has effective processes for accurately assessing the relative importance (potential future value) of various intellectual capital bundles.

Ninteenth: make sure that your company has holistic business processes in place for managing the risk to the company's own proprietary information and its business partners' proprietary information in the normal course of business. Make sure joint ventures, joint and co-development work, consortiums, university relationships, and other non-standard buying and selling relationships are covered. Third party management of your company's intellectual capital should be included in the scope of this.

Twentieth: study your company's quality management discipline. Become proficient in the use of its vocabulary and tools. Use them to build and improve business processes in the realm of intellectual capital management through cross-enterprise teams.

Twenty-First: get serious about change management and communication. Get experts in these areas to consult with you regularly and help you plan and manage your change management and communication programs.

Twenty-Second: where you can and where beneficial, support the development of audit programs in the field of intellectual capital management. Be careful here. Do not allow your office to be perceived as the intellectual capital management police. If this happens, your work is doomed.

Twenty-Third: where you can and where beneficial, support the development of metrics, organizational objectives, and personal objectives associated with excellence in intellectual capital management. Again, be careful here. You do not want your office to be perceived as the intellectual capital management police.

Twenty-Fourth: become professionally expert at the valuation of intellectual capital rights, whether protected by intellectual property law or contract law or not and whether technology based, business process based, relationship based, know-how based, or intangible product and services based. This expertise is at the heart of your unique value proposition to the company.

Wrap-up and Call to Action

Lately, after kindly reading a version of the manuscript that preceded this book, another friend suggested that I add more personal stories and write about my feelings as I've navigated the various companies that I've worked for and as I've developed my practice concerning intellectual capital management. Let me tell you, this journey has been a bit of a tester. A bit of an adventure. Lots of people really don't want to hear certain information. And apparently, some have not wanted to hear certain information from me, in particular.

Yes, there are many interesting stories, many odd excursions into the psychology of our species. Some of them are big dollar stories. Some are smaller dollar stories. However, many of the smaller dollar stories turned out to be wonderful just-in-time-mentoring opportunities that I prefer to believe forestalled future big dollar problems. All of them built and reinforced an alliance network throughout the company.

Most of these stories are proprietary and would be recognizable—even if I genericized them—to people who I regard or have regarded as work friends. People whom I admire and respect. And not all would be happy, if I told these stories truthfully, after reading them. Some would take such stories as criticisms. Others would take my telling them in so public a way as a betrayal of trust.

In any event, most of these stories are here, distilled to their essence, the identifying particulars boiled away. The ideas—the suggested approaches to various aspects of intellectual capital management—are the distillate. In other words, the overwhelming majority of what I speak of here is the result of research in the field. Many of the approaches have been field tested and shown to work. These notes record the results. The little that has not been field tested has—in my view—a high probability of success, if applied at the appropriate point in an enterprise's journey toward excellence in intellectual capital management and with the appropriate buy-in from leadership.

(But every company is a little or maybe a lot different from the companies I've worked for. So, exactly which of the ideas I've suggested are most effective and helpful will depend on you, your company's organizational structure, its business models, the role intellectual capital plays in its value proposition, the personalities of the company's leaders, where you are placed in the organization, the organization's internal political relationships, and its culture. I'm confident that not all of these ideas will be equally useful or acceptable in your particular circumstance. But you be the judge.)

The few anecdotes I have recounted are offered obliquely. Maybe that means that these notes are less interesting to read, since as we all know, fully fleshed stories of various sorts can be endlessly fascinating. Again, so be it.

I've been privileged to work with some stellar people who mostly were trying to do the right thing. Yes, there have been some organizational terrorists and some psychological guerillas. But you know what? No big deal, in the long arc of history. I have proceeded successfully with much of what I'm suggesting here, without too much intense or prolonged suffering. The evidence, the logic, the effectiveness of what this program is about can be compelling, if implemented with verified evidence, patience, perseverance, a collaborative spirit, a cross-enterprise initiative or set of initiatives, and a little organizational and psychological jiu jitsu.

You know jiu jitsu, don't you, metaphorically speaking? You use the opponent's force against him rather than confronting it with one's own force. Oh, occasionally one does need to apply another technique. But this is an extremely rare circumstance. In most cases, collegial cooperation combined with some friendly jiu jitsu will work beautifully.

What was the advice that Ruth Bader Ginsberg received from her mother-in-law? To nurture a successful marriage, it helps to be a little bit deaf. Or something like that. So too with our work to improve intellectual capital management. It does help to be a little bit deaf and to treat our colleagues with the respect they very much deserve. Then we must go about our business, doing our work for the organization and bringing our colleagues along, gradually. After all, this is the way significant beneficial change of all kinds happens—gradually, and often, after what seems like an epoch, suddenly. It's a slow-motion sport, for the most part.

What's important here is that we get going. That we get ourselves organized and focused properly on the source of most of the value in companies today: intellectual capital. That we stop blundering around so much and start collaborating on what needs to be done, what the priorities are, and who will do what. And when I say "we," I mean business-people who have some familiarity with what intellectual capital is and how it works, what role it plays in enterprises, how valuable it really is, despite what the finance and accounting people put in their textbooks, and despite what many business people think today. By "we," I mean you, dear reader. And me.

How do we do that? Well, for starters, we need to share a common sense of urgency, a common understanding of the issues, the subject matter, and companies' opportunities and vulnerabilities. Without this, we will get nowhere.

Next, we need a common vocabulary, because if we don't agree on and use a common vocabulary, we will continue to talk past each other, contributing confusion to the chaos, and the business-people who have no particular expertise in intellectual capital management and little awareness of what it is will continue to have no idea how to think about this stuff. They'll dismiss us all as a bunch of pseudo-intellectual-capital-management cake eaters.

We are headed in the right direction. Let's keep going, resolving issues and developing consensus. A conference or two or three may be in order here to nail this down. The language I use here is just one person's take.

I'm happy to move to a different vocabulary or a modification of this vocabulary, as long as we clear up the issues raised earlier. Whatever that vocabulary is needs to be simple to explain, simple to understand, actionable, and business/financial rather than legal in its orientation.

Finally, we need a profession to call home, a group of like-minded people who will band together to sort this all out and then kick out the jams. We need a profession that is focused on supporting the strategic business objectives of most companies, which are products-and-services-oriented. We need a profession that views itself as not only providing expertise to "IP businesses" but also to products and services businesses.

Without a profession to call home, those of us who understand something about intellectual capital and who are focused on products and services businesses in our practice (and there are probably tens of thousands of us, at this point) will likely continue to wander in the wilderness.

How do you construct a profession? Well, you need a body of literature that poses and attempts to answer questions that are important and that are particular to the practice of that profession. You need methodologies. You need standards. You need research. You would normally expect to be supported within an academic discipline across most business schools. You would expect a professional association to support you, through the provision of appropriate content in conferences, webinars, and courses.

We have some of this, but we need much, much more.

Acknowledgements

There are several generous friends and work colleagues who prepared me to write and coached me in the writing of this compendium of Woody wisdom, and I want to thank them.

First, I want to thank two colleagues who worked with me and stuck by me through the yelling and screaming phases of change management, as well as the more serene moments: Julia Klaren and Carolyn Tomberlin. They routinely told me when I was off my tree bark and kept our rollicking formation flight aloft, providing energy, discipline, innovation, courage, insight, organization, and inspiration, in equal measures, along the way.

I want to thank Robin Corwin especially for her many excellent contributions to the policies and processes of managing intellectual capital better and for her heroic contributions to LES Standards.

I want to thank Rik Powell especially for his contributions to intellectual capital management collaboration across organizational boundaries.

Thanks to Jackie Pelland, an expert on leadership and change management, who is responsible for teaching me almost everything I think I know on both subjects.

I want to thank Tanya Moore, Mary Adams, Pam Demain, Ken Wilson, Scott Williams, Mihaela Bojin, Bob Goldman, Ken Jarboe, Kevin Arst, Ron Laurie, Gillian Fenton, and Mike Pellegrino—friends and colleagues who read and commented on earlier drafts of these notes, providing excellent suggestions for their improvement.

I want to thank Paul Roberts for his excellent feedback on the manuscript and his insightful and generous Foreword to this book.

I also want to thank Mary Adams, Kevin Arst, Mihaela Bojin, Gillian Fenton, Ron Laurie, and Scott Williams for their very kind endorsements.

Thanks also to Bob Raeside, who several years ago sat me down at a party in an airplane hangar and told me I should write a book. What—I wanted to know—do you think I should write about? You'll figure it out, he said.

I want to thank Carla Blackman and her team at Design Interface for their excellent support and deep knowledge about book design and publishing matters. And thank you to David Drews for his excellent help in making sure I sound like I know what I'm talking about.

The field research that is distilled here was made possible by the leaders in the various companies in which I have worked over the past 40 years, and I want to thank the scores and scores of them for their forbearance, support, and encouragement.

Finally, thanks to the members of LES and LES Standards, whose friendships and support have been critical to my mustering the temerity to voice a few thoughts on the field of intellectual capital management.

Author Biography

Bill's career in three Fortune 500 companies, a startup, and now in his consulting company—Mind IC LLC—has been in the field of intellectual capital management. His focus has been on creating, uncovering, protecting, and extracting the value of companies' intellectual capital. His expertise is in diverse areas of intellectual capital management: business cadre leadership, rights valuation, rights strategy, public policy, enterprise policy and process, transactions, patent protection, standards, and

Bill Elkington

change management across the enterprise. He is a former president and chair of the Licensing Executives Society (LES), USA and Canada, and is the former chair of the LES Standards Board. He has published many articles on the subject of intellectual capital management and has been a frequent speaker at conferences and on webinars in the field. He can be reached at: bill.mindic@outlook.com.

CPSIA information can be obtained
at www.ICGtesting.com
Printed in the USA
BVHW032352300121
599037BV00004B/13